Father Orengo, one of the early missionaries to Tennessee

Amen, LET'S EAT!

A Collection of Recipes from members of the Serra Club of Williamson County, and friends and supporters of Serra

All proceeds from the sale of this cookbook will directly support seminarian education in the Diocese of Nashville, Tennessee

May, 2013

Copyright © Serra Club of Williamson County, Tennessee

All rights reserved.

Cover design: Jeff Carroll

Interior design: Margie Thessin

Back cover photo of Bishop David R. Choby with several seminarians: The Tennessee Register

Historic photos: Kim Hoover

Food photos: Istock

Cookbook committee: Betty Jo Allen, Missy Rudman, Jeanette Teague and Margie Thessin

A hearty thank you to everyone who submitted a recipe. In doing so, you are supporting our wonderful seminarians in the diocese of Nashville.

Every effort has been made to assure the accuracy of these recipes, and to include all recipes that were submitted. Any errors are inadvertent. Should you find an error or omission, please contact Margie Thessin at themargie@comcast.net.

ISBN: 1484037936

EAN-13: 978-1484037935

Contents

Foreword	7
Beverages	9
Appetizers	13
Bread	27
Brunch	37
Soups	47
Salads	61
Vegetables and Side Dishes	79
Pasta	99
Main Courses	
Poultry	109
Pork	128
Beef	134
Lamb	144
Seafood	146
Desserts	155
History of the Catholic Church in Williamson County	193
Index	201

Foreword

SERRA, founded in 1935 by four Catholic laymen from Seattle, was named for our Patron, Padre Junipero Serra, a Franciscan missionary priest who founded 9 of the 19 missions in California. Since then, Serra has expanded to 43 countries throughout the world, having some 22,000 members.

The mission of Serra is twofold: to encourage and affirm vocations to the priesthood and vowed religious life; and to grow in our own spiritual faith. With the support of Father Edward Arnold, long-time pastor at St. Philip, we formed the Serra Club of Williamson County in November, 2004, beginning with 27 members, and growing to 94 in 2013. God has truly blessed us!

This cookbook, compiled by our lady Serrans, is to help raise funds to support our programs and projects. The men of Serra have volunteered to be the "samplers" of their efforts, tasting the recipes they have put together!

Our cause is truly a noble one. What greater gift could we give our Church than to help plant the seed in a young man or woman to consider God's call to become a priest or religious. Like the proverbial stone dropped into a placid lake, the ripples each priest or religious produces will touch countless lives, hopefully bringing many to Christ and His Church.

Our heartfelt thanks to our lady Serrans for furthering the mission of Serra through their hard work in putting this book together. May God bless their work in His Vineyard!

Sincerely in Christ,

Lloyd P. Crockett

Charter Member, Serra Club of Williamson County

Past President, Serra International Board of Trustees

Beverages

AWESOME ICED TEA PUNCH

1 gal. water
4 family-size tea bags
2 2/3 cup sugar
1 cup lemon juice
1 ½ cup orange juice
Handful of mint leaves
2 liter ginger ale

Boil water. Steep tea bags and mint for 10 to 15 minutes. Add sugar; stir to dissolve. Strain. Add lemon juice, orange juice. Chill very, very well. When ready to serve add ginger ale.

Judy Tujague

EGG NOG

12 eggs, separated
1 cup sugar
1 cup milk
2 cups whiskey
6 cups heavy cream
Nutmeg

Separate the eggs and stir yolks till well blended. Whip the egg whites till stiff and then whip the cream. Add everything together, except the nutmeg. Chill overnight. When serving, grate the nutmeg atop the eggnog in the glass.

Margie Thessin

MICHELLE'S VODKA SLUSH

1 qt. vodka
2 lg. cans orange juice concentrate
2 med. cans lemonade concentrate
11 cups water
2 cups sugar
3 Tbsp. instant tea
2 liters 7-Up

Freeze 7-Up in ring mold. Dissolve sugar and tea in 3 to 4 cups of water. Add rest of ingredients and freeze. Take out in time to slush. Add ring.

Judy Tujague

MOCHA PUNCH

This punch recipe is one I made for Moms R Us at St. Philip about a century ago—it was a real hit—no doubt due to the caffeine and sugar!

6 cups water
½ cup Nestles Quik chocolate drink mix
½ cup sugar
¼ cup instant coffee granules
½ cup vanilla ice cream
½ gal. chocolate ice cream
1 cup heavy whipping cream, whipped
Chocolate curls or shavings from milk chocolate bar

In a large saucepan, bring water to a boil. Remove from heat. Add drink mix, sugar and coffee and whisk until dissolved. Cover and refrigerate 4 hours or overnight. About 30 minutes before serving, pour chocolate mixture into a large punch bowl. Add ice cream by the scoopfuls and stir until partially melted. Garnish with whipped cream and chocolate shavings, if desired.

Jenny Turner

SANGRIA

1-1.75-liter bottle of red wine, either Burgundy or Lambrusco
¼ cup brandy
¼ cup vodka
¼ cup Triple Sec or other orange liqueur
1 28 oz. club soda or other carbonated water, chilled
1 orange, cut in half and sliced
1 apple, cut in wedges

Chill orange for garnish (apple does not need to be chilled). Mix wine, brandy, vodka, Triple Sec in a pitcher or bowl. Chill.

Just before serving, add carbonated water. Add orange and apple wedges to the mix or use an orange wedge for the glass rim, insert an apple wedge to a skewer and use as stirrer.

Ana Anaya

FRUIT TEA

6 small tea bags
4 cups boiling water
1 ½ cup sugar
1 -6 oz. can frozen orange juice concentrate
1 -6 oz, can frozen lemonade concentrate
10 cups water

Place tea bags in boiling water. Let steep 5 minutes. Add sugar, stir until dissolved. Add remaining ingredients. Stir until well mixed.

Nena Manci

WHISKEY SOUR PUNCH SLUSH

2- 12 oz. cans frozen lemonade
1- 12. oz cans frozen orange juice
7- 12 oz. cans water
1 qt. bourbon
2 pkg. frozen strawberries

Mix and freeze in shallow container, no more than 3 to 4 inches deep. Remove from freezer 1 to 2 hours before serving.

Judy Tujague

Appetizers

ARTICHOKE-CHEESE PUFFS

I found this recipe on a box of Ritz Crackers.

6-8 whole wheat Ritz Crackers
1-8 oz. pkg. cream cheese, softened
¼ cup Parmesan cheese, grated
¼ cup mozzarella cheese, shredded
½ cup canned artichoke hearts, chopped and drained

Crush crackers and place crumbs in a shallow bowl. Mix cheese and artichoke until well blended. Shape into 32 balls using 2 teaspoons of cheese mixture for each ball. Coat with crumbs. Place in a single layer in container. Refrigerate at least 30 minutes or overnight (can be stored in refrigerator for up to 24 hours). Heat oven to 350°. Place whole Ritz Crackers on baking sheet. Top each with a cheese ball. Bake 10 minutes or until heated through.

Donna DeCoster

CHEDDAR CHEESE BALL

1 lb. sharp cheddar cheese, grated
1 cup mayonnaise
1 small onion, grated
Black pepper to taste
Dash cayenne pepper
1 cup pecans, chopped
Small jar strawberry jam

Blend first six ingredients and shape into round ball, slightly flattened on top. Refrigerate to chill. When ready to serve, top with strawberry jam. Serve with crackers. My favorite crackers with this are Nabisco Triscuits.

Shelby Boyd

AUNTIE ANN'S COPYCAT PRETZELS

3½ cup warm water
1⅛ tsp. active yeast
2 Tbsp. brown sugar
1⅛ tsp. salt
1 cup bread flour

3 cups flour
2 cups warm water
2 Tbsp. baking soda
Kosher salt, to taste
2-4 Tbsp. butter, melted

Sprinkle yeast on 1½ cups lukewarm water in mixing bowl; stir to dissolve. Add sugar and salt; stir to dissolve then add flour and knead dough until smooth and elastic. Let rise at least 30 minutes. While dough is rising, prepare a baking soda water bath with remaining warm water and the baking soda. Be certain to stir often. After dough has risen, pinch off bits of dough and roll into a long rope (about ½ inch or less thick) and shape. Dip pretzel into soda solution and place on greased baking sheet. Allow pretzels to rise again. Bake in a 450 degree preheated oven for about 10 minutes or until golden. Brush with melted butter, sprinkle with salt and enjoy!

Ashley Blackburn

BLACK BEAN SALSA

1 Tbsp. granulated sugar
½ cup apple cider vinegar
½ cup olive oil
1 tsp. salt
½ tsp. fresh black ground pepper
2-11 oz. cans white shoepeg corn, drained

14 oz. can black beans, rinsed and drained
1 bunch green onions, sliced
½ cup fresh cilantro, chopped
½ cup red bell pepper, chopped
1 container crumbled feta cheese

In a medium saucepan, add sugar, vinegar, olive oil, salt and pepper. Bring to a simmer, stirring until sugar is dissolved. Set aside to cool. In a medium bowl, add corn, black beans, green onions, cilantro, bell pepper and feta cheese; set aside. Pour vinegar/oil mixture over vegetables. Chill about 8 hours. Serve as a salad or as an appetizer with tortilla chips. Makes a large quantity!

Jeanette Teague

BREAD AND BUTTER PICKLES

6 lbs. cucumbers
2 garlic cloves
1½ cup sliced onion
⅓ cup salt
1-2 quarts ice, crushed or cubed
1½ tsp. celery seed
4½ cups sugar
2 Tbsp. mustard seed
1½ tsp. turmeric
3 cups white vinegar

Wash cucumbers thoroughly, using vegetable brush. Slice unpeeled cucumbers into ⅛-¼ in. slices. Add onions, garlic and salt. Cover with ice. Mix thoroughly. Allow to stand for 3 hours. Drain thoroughly and remove garlic. Combine sugar, spices and vinegar. Heat just to a boil. Add cucumber and onion slices. Heat 5 minutes. Pack loosely into clean, hot pint jars. Adjust lids. Process in boiling water bath for 5 minutes.

Ruth Ann Graveno

CRAB SPREAD

2 Tbsp. Worcestershire sauce
2 Tbsp. mayonnaise
1 Tbsp. lemon juice
Garlic salt to taste
½ onion, grated
12 oz. cream cheese
⅓ bottle chili sauce
½ lb. lump crabmeat

Mix first 6 ingredients by hand or in food processor. Spread mixture in a 9-inch serving dish. Refrigerate until firm. Just before serving, cover with layer of chili sauce and top completely with crabmeat. Sprinkle with parsley. Serve with crackers.

Judy Tujague

COWBOY CAVIAR

2 -15 oz. cans black-eyed peas, drained and rinsed
¼ cup extra-virgin olive oil
¼ cup red wine vinegar
¼ cup sugar or Splenda
1 tsp. garlic, chopped
½ red bell pepper, cored, seeded and finely chopped
½ green bell pepper, cored, seeded and finely chopped
¼ red onion, chopped
Juice of 1 lime
Kosher salt and freshly ground black pepper to taste
¼ cup roughly chopped cilantro (optional)
1 serrano or jalapeno chili, stemmed, seeded and finely chopped (optional)

Combine oil, vinegar and sugar (or Splenda) in a small pan on stove. Heat until combined. Combine beans, cilantro, garlic, chilies, bell peppers and onion in a large bowl. Pour cooled oil and vinegar mixture over bean mixture. Squeeze in lime.
Toss well and refrigerate for several hours or overnight. Adjust salt and pepper to taste.
Serve with pita chips or scoops.

Teresa A. Jones

CREAM CHEESE AND PINEAPPLE BALL

8 oz. cream cheese, softened
1 sm. can crushed pineapple, drained
2 Tbsp. green pepper, chopped
2 Tbsp. green onion, finely chopped
1 tsp. Worcestershire sauce
Salt and pepper to taste
¾ cup pecans, chopped and crushed

Mix all above except pecans. Form into a ball and roll in crushed pecans. Refrigerate. Serve with your favorite crackers. Delicious!

Diane Serfass

FIESTA BEAN SALAD (OR DIP)

Our family has made this for years. It is colorful and delicious and very easy to throw together. It was originally known as a salad, but we only eat it scooped with tortilla chips. Easy to double for a party or big family.

1 can black beans, rinsed and drained
1 can corn, drained
1 can diced tomatoes, drained
1 large onion, diced
1 large green pepper, diced
½ bottle of Kraft Catalina (not Lite) dressing

Mix these all together and serve with tortilla chips. This is even better after chilling to meld flavors.

Erin Morel

GOAT CHEESE-PEAR PANCETTA CRISPS

There won't be a miss with this one. Everyone, including children, seems to love this little appetizer. Easy to make and delicious.

12 slices pancetta (about ½ lb.)
1 pear
4 oz. goat cheese, crumbled
Fresh pepper
Honey

Arrange pancetta slices in a single layer on a parchment-lined baking sheet. Bake at 450° for 8 to 10 minutes or until crisp. Transfer to a paper towel-lined wire rack. Let stand 10 minutes. Slice or core pear. Cut pear crosswise into 12 thin rings. Arrange on a serving platter. Top evenly with pancetta and goat cheese; sprinkle with pepper. Drizzle with honey. Garnish if desired.

Gwen Perkins, Chapman's II

HUMMUS WITH A TWIST

½ cup canola oil
2 garlic cloves
Juice of 1 lemon
1 Tbsp. Dijon mustard
1 cup cooked chickpeas
3 Tbsp. tahini
¾ cup extra-virgin olive oil, plus more for garnish
¼ cup small ice cubes
Salt
1½ ripe avocados, halved and pitted
Sea salt

In a small saucepan, bring the canola oil and garlic to a very slow simmer over low heat. Simmer gently until the garlic is tender, about 20 minutes. Drain the garlic and either discard the oil or save it for another use.

In the bowl of a food processor fitted with a steel blade attachment, combine the garlic with the juice of half the lemon and the mustard. Pulse until smooth. Add the chickpeas and, with the motor running, drizzle in the tahini, then ½ cup of the olive oil. Add the ice cubes and pulse until smooth. Season with salt and transfer the chickpea mixture to a medium bowl.

Add the avocado and remaining lemon juice to the bowl of the food processor. Pulse while drizzling in the remaining ¼ cup olive oil until smooth. Season with salt, then transfer to the bowl and fold into the chickpea puree.

Transfer the hummus to a serving bowl. Garnish with a drizzle of olive oil and sea salt before serving with desired accompaniments.

Terry Bies

KIELBASA BITES

18 oz. beer
1- 18 oz. bottle barbeque sauce
½ cup brown sugar
¼ cup Dijon mustard
3 lbs. kielbasa, cut into ½ inch pieces

Combine all ingredients except kielbasa in a large skillet over medium heat. Bring to a boil, stirring occasionally. Reduce to low and add kielbasa until browned and glazed, about 1 hour.

Judy Tujague

MUSHROOMS

I serve these at parties and everyone loves them. Enjoy!

3 lbs. mushrooms, washed with damp paper towel.
¾ cup unsalted butter
3 cups red wine (always use a good wine that you would drink)
¾ tsp. dill weed
1 tsp. ground pepper
¾ tsp. garlic powder
2 cups boiling water
2 beef cubes
2 chicken cubes
2 tsp. olive oil
2 tsp. Worcestershire sauce

Combine all ingredients in a large pan and cook for several hours with lid on. Take lid off and let them slow boil until the liquid cooks down. You will want to leave some liquid. Remember that mushrooms cook down so if you are having a large crowd you will need to increase the recipe.

Betty Jo Allen

MEME'S CHEESE BALL

Easy and good. Enjoy!

2 – 8 oz. pkg. cream cheese
1 jar Kraft Old English cheese spread
1 jar Kraft pimento cheese spread
2 Tbsp. Worcestershire sauce
1 very small onion, chopped
Bag of pecans, chopped

Place all ingredients in a bowl except the pecans. Mix all together into the shape of a ball. Place on a plate and cover. Refrigerate several hours to overnight. Spread pecans on wax paper and roll the cheese ball in the pecans.

Cecelia Inman

MJ'S SOUTHWESTERN LAYERED DIP

This is my family's version of this popular appetizer.

1-16 oz. can refried beans
¼ cup mild red peppers, chopped
¼ cup fresh cilantro, chopped
1-7 oz. can corn, drained
⅓ cup green olives with pimentos, sliced
1 cup mayonnaise
1 pkg. taco seasoning mix (hotness to your taste)
½ cup taco-seasoned shredded cheese (or your choice)
Tortilla chips

Spread refried beans in a deep 9-inch pie plate. Sprinkle most of the chopped red peppers over beans; top with most of the cilantro. Scatter the drained corn and follow with the chopped olives. Combine mayonnaise and taco seasoning mix; spread evenly over all. Sprinkle with cheese, then scatter remaining cilantro and red peppers on top. Chill if not served immediately. Serve with chips.

Marni Johnson

PAM'S DIP 2-1-1-1-1-1

2 cups sour cream	1 Tbsp. parsley
1 cup mayonnaise	1 Tbsp. minced onion
1 Tbsp. dill weed	1 Tbsp. seasoned salt

Mix. Refrigerate overnight. Serve with veggies and pretzels.

Mary Grindstaff

PARTY MEATBALLS

These are a favorite at my Christmas party.

Large bag of Italian meatballs (I buy a bag of 100 at Costco)
1-16 oz. bottle meatless spaghetti sauce
3 jars honey barbecue sauce
1 large can pineapple juice
½ cup brown sugar

Mix spaghetti sauce, barbecue sauce, pineapple juice and brown sugar, then add meatballs. I use my crock pot and place on high for about 1 hour and then turn to low for about 5 hours.

Betty Jo Allen

POP JOE'S GRANOLA

½ cup oil	1½ cup walnuts, chopped
½ cup honey	1½ cup pecans or almonds, chopped
1 tsp. vanilla	
1 cup water	1½ cup sunflower seeds, hulled
1 lg. box old fashioned Quaker oats	

Mix oil, honey, vanilla and water. Then add to remaining ingredients. Spread thinly on several cookie sheets. Bake at 270° for 45 minutes, turning occasionally until golden. Cool and store in air-tight container or may be frozen. Serve with fresh fruit.

Joe Reynolds

REMOULADE SAUCE

This comes from Saia's Restaurant in Kenner, Louisiana

1 cup mayonnaise
¼ cup Creole mustard
¼ cup chili sauce
⅛ cup white vinegar
⅛ cup horseradish
⅛ cup sweet relish
1 stalk celery, minced
2 stalks green onion, minced
¼ cup onion, minced
¼ Tbsp. Lea & Perrins Worcestershire sauce
2 drops Tabasco

Mix all ingredients. Chill. Use as a dip for shrimp and veggies. Salad dressing is another option. Layer in small bowl some lettuce, shrimp, remoulade and fresh lemon.

Elly Brantley

SENSATIONAL STUFFED MUSHROOMS

I am submitting this in honor of Sharon Wilson who first submitted it to the Moms R Us Cookbook that St. Philip moms published in the early '90's! We still use it for special occasions, such as Daddy Mc's birthday when we don't know what else to get him.

1 lb. med. mushrooms	½ cup Parmesan cheese, grated
Butter	
1- 8 oz. pkg. cream cheese	1 Tbsp. green onions, chopped

Remove mushroom stems, chop enough stems to make ½ cup. Cook mushroom caps in butter for 5 minutes. Combine cream cheese and parmesan cheese, mixing until well blended. Add chopped stems and onion, mix well. Fill mushroom caps; broil until golden brown.

Erin Morel

SPINACH AND MUSHROOM ON CROSTINI

12 button mushrooms, cleaned and sliced
1 pkg. frozen spinach leaves (without sauce)
3 large shallots, sliced thinly
¼ -½ cup Parmesan cheese, grated
¼ cup Port or Marsala wine
2 garlic cloves, chopped fine
2 Tbsp. extra virgin olive oil
1 Tbsp. unsalted butter
Pinch salt and pepper
A loaf of French bread or a baguette

Thaw spinach, squeeze water from leaves and wrap in paper towel to reserve.

Heat fry pan with olive oil. Add shallots to sauté in fry pan. Add the garlic to the fry pan and continue to sauté. Add sliced mushrooms to the fry pan with the shallots.

Add the Port or Marsala. Add the butter. Remove the above when done to a large mixing bowl. Add the spinach leaves to the mixing bowl and incorporate all the ingredients.

Add the Parmesan cheese to the bowl and mix with the mushrooms and spinach. Slice the bread on the bias and place each slice on a baking sheet. Ladle the spinach mix on top of each piece.

Place in heated oven at 325° for approximately 15 minutes or until "toasty." Remove and sprinkle with a little more Parmesan cheese

Serve on your favorite platter as an appetizer and be sure to have a little chilled Burgundy or Chardonnay available.

Bill Kennedy

ROSEMARY CRACKERS

1¾ cup blanched almond flour
½ tsp. sea salt
1 Tbsp. fresh rosemary, finely chopped
1 Tbsp. olive oil
1 egg

Mix all together. Roll out between two pieces of wax paper. Bake at 350° for 12-15 minutes on parchment paper. Cut into squares with a pizza cutter and enjoy! If you don't like rosemary, use cocoa powder and some sort of sweetener like honey to make a little sweeter cracker. I've also flavored with just lemon rind.

Holly Moore

TRAIL MIX

MIX
3 cups Cheerios
1 box Wheat Chex
¾ box Rice Chex
¾ box Corn Chex
1 can peanuts
1 lb. pretzels
1 lb. whole cashews
1 lb. pecans
1 large can mixed nuts

HEAT ON STOVE
1 Tbsp. Worcestershire sauce
1 Tbsp. celery salt
1 Tbsp. garlic powder
1 Tbsp. onion powder
3 sticks butter

Pour over cereal and nut mixture, and then transfer to a large pan. Bake 1 hour at 225°, mixing every 15 minutes.

Ashley Blackburn

VIDALIA ONION DIP

Yummy and SOOOO easy! I had this at the home of a friend in Magnolia Springs, AL. She got the recipe from Kraftfoods.com.

2 Cups Kraft Real mayonnaise
1- 8 oz. pkg. Kraft Natural Italian Cheese Crumbles
1 large Vidalia or Walla Walla onion, coarsely chopped (about 2 cups)

Preheat oven to 375°. Mix all ingredients until well blended. Spread into 8-inch square baking dish. Bake 30 minutes or until golden brown. Cool slightly. Serve with Triscuit crackers.

Fran Greene

VIETNAMESE EGG ROLLS

1 lb. ground pork
½ pound peeled shrimp
3 chopped garlic cloves
1 carrot, peeled and shredded
¼ cabbage, shredded
2 oz. dried vermicelli noodles
1 oz. dried black fungus/cloud ear mushrooms
2-3 large eggs
Ground black pepper
2-3 tbsp of fish sauce (depending on taste)
Egg roll wrappers – 12 oz package (30-50 rice paper sheets, 10 inch diameter)
Frying oil, vegetable, corn, canola or peanut

Soak vermicelli noodles and mushrooms in a bowl of warm water for 20 minutes. In a food processor pulse-grind shrimp, garlic until roughly chopped. Add to mixture, drained vermicelli noodles and mushrooms, pulse-grind briefly until all ingredients are integrated.

In a large mixing bowl, transfer ingredients from food processor and combine with ground meat and shredded vegetables. Add black pepper, fish sauce, and 2 eggs. Use hands to mix ingredients together. If the mixture seems dry, add the other egg.

To wrap the rolls with rice paper, fill a shallow dish with 1 inch of warm water. Quickly dip rice paper in the water bath, making sure all parts of the paper are wet. Place wet rice paper on a clean dish towel/plate and let it soften. Once it is soft and pliable, peel it off the towel and place on to a plate. Lay 1½ tablespoon of filling on the lower edge of the rice paper, near you, leaving 1 inch edge. Begin to fold egg roll like an envelope: first, fold over the lower 1 inch edge over the filing, then the left edge, then the right edge. Now roll the roll up to the top edge. Place the wrapped egg roll on a platter and keep on rolling!

Heat the oil in a large, deep frying pan over medium high heat. Test the oil by dipping the tip of a wooden spoon or wooden chop stick – if it bubbles around the tip then the oil is ready. Place egg roll one at a time into hot oil, with the seam down (this will keep it from unraveling) and then quickly turn the egg roll to ensure the skin crisps up and does not stick to other egg rolls in the pan. Adjust heat so that the oil is bubbling gently and not too vigorously around the egg rolls. Each egg roll will take about 5 minutes to cook – golden brown spots and skin is super crispy. Shake the egg roll over the pan to help remove the excess oil. Place egg roll on layers of paper towels to drain.

Fr. Tien Tran

BAKED ZUCCHINI

3 cups zucchini, thinly sliced
1 cup Bisquick
½ cup onion, chopped
½ cup Parmesan cheese
½ cup vegetable oil
4 eggs beaten

2 tbs. parsley
½ tbs. salt
½ tsp. pepper
½ tsp. oregano
½ tsp. chopped garlic

Mix all ingredients together. Heat oven to 350°. Grease 9 x 13-inch pan and pour in zucchini mixture. Bake 25 minutes or until golden brown. Cut into 2 x 1-inch pieces and serve hot.

Tracy Barnes

Breads

BISCOTTI

This recipe was given to me by a cousin of mine, Louise Battisti about 35 years ago. She lived in my home town, Ambridge, Pa. She used to sell them in different specialty stores.

1 cup almonds, chopped	1 cup sugar
3 cups all-purpose flour	⅓ cup vegetable oil
1 Tbsp. baking powder	3 eggs
¼ tsp. nutmeg	1 tsp. vanilla extract
1 stick of margarine (room temperature)	1 tsp. almond extract

Heat oven to 350°. Prepare 2 cookie sheets by lining with parchment paper. Heat almonds in oven for few minutes while oven is heating then put aside until after dough is mixed. Mix flour, baking powder and nutmeg and place in bowl; set aside. In your mixer, add margarine, sugar and oil. Mix together on medium speed, adding eggs one at a time. Add vanilla and almond extracts. Add flour mixture gradually. Dough will be very soft but do not add additional flour. Add chopped almonds.

With a large spoon, divide dough into 4 parts. Take ¼ of the dough and shape into logs crosswise on the sheet. You should be able to get two logs on each cookie sheet. Each log should be 4 x 11 inches. Bake at 350° for 15 to 20 minutes till light brown.

Take out and let logs cool. Then slice each log diagonally into ½ inch slices. Lay slices down on the cookie sheet and toast till light brown, about 5 minutes on each side.

Remove on rack to cool. Store in tightly covered container.

Louise Volpe

BANANA BREAD

2 cups flour
2 tsp. baking soda
1 tsp. salt
1 cup butter

2 cups sugar
2 cups mashed banana
4 eggs
1 cup nuts, chopped

Cream butter and sugar. Add banana. Add eggs. Add dry ingredients. Bake at 350° for 20 minutes for muffins and 55 minutes for 2 loaves.

Meb Tujague

COFFEE CAKE

This is a very good cake.

CAKE
1 box yellow cake mix
(without pudding)
¾ cup water
¾ cup oil
1 pkg. instant vanilla pudding
4 eggs

1 tsp. vanilla
1 tsp. butter flavoring
½ cup sugar
4 tsp. cinnamon
¼ cup pecans

Beat cake mix, water, oil, pudding, eggs, vanilla and butter flavoring for 6 to 8 minutes. Mix sugar, cinnamon and pecans separately. Pour cake mix in a greased and floured Bundt pan a small amount at a time and alternatively with a small amount of the sugar, cinnamon and pecan mixture. Bake in a Bundt pan at 325-350°. Cool in pan for 8 minutes.

GLAZE
1 cup powdered sugar
3 Tbsp. milk
1 tsp. vanilla
1 tsp. butter flavoring

Jean M. Berry

COFFEE CRESCENTS

This is my mother's recipe. It is made with yeast but the dough is easy to work with and the crescents are delicious. It is a family favorite particularly at Christmas time.

ROLLS
1 pkg. dry yeast
1 tsp. salt
¼ cup lukewarm water
1 cup butter or margarine
4 cups flour
¾ cups cold milk
1 Tbsp. sugar
3 egg yolks, beaten

FILLING
3 (or 4) egg whites
1 cup chopped nuts
1 cup sugar
Cinnamon

Activate yeast in lukewarm water plus a pinch of the sugar. Set aside. Combine the rest of the dry ingredients. Cut in margarine. Combine yeast mixture, milk and egg yolks. Add to the flour mixture. Knead to smooth dough.

Cover dough and refrigerate several hours or overnight. Divide dough into four parts. Roll ¼ inch think on pastry cloth. Beat egg whites until stiff. Add sugar gradually. Spread ¼ of egg white mixture on each piece of dough. Sprinkle with cinnamon and nuts. Roll dough up by lifting pastry cloth. Seal edges with water. Place seam-side down on cookie sheet and form into crescent shape.

Cover and let rise in warm place until double in size, about 1 to 1½ hours. Bake at 325° for 20 to 30 minutes or until lightly browned. Ice while warm with powdered sugar icing.

Donna DeCoster

CORN BREAD MUFFINS

This goes great with chili.

1 cup yellow self-rising corn meal
½ tsp. salt
¼ cup oil
1- 8 oz. can cream corn
1 cup sour cream
2 eggs
1 Tbsp. sugar

Mix ingredients. Drop in greased muffin tins or mini tins. Bake at 400° for 25 minutes (less if making mini muffins)

Marie Morris

FOOL PROOF SOUTHERN BISCUITS

I tried all kinds of biscuit recipes, with not much success, until I found this one.

4 cups flour
2 heaping Tbsp. baking powder
1 cup shortening
1½ cup buttermilk (or 1½ Tbsp. vinegar, then fill measuring cup to 1½ cup milk)

Mix flour and baking powder in to a large bowl. Cut in shortening. Add buttermilk and mix with a wooden spoon. Knead dough lightly on floured board. Roll out to a ½ inch thickness and cut into rounds. Bake at 450° for 12 minutes. Cooked biscuits may be frozen or dough may be refrigerated for 2 days.

Nancy Tuberty

IRISH SODA BREAD

Easy for that St. Patty's Day Breakfast!

2 cups all purpose flour, sifted
½ tsp. baking soda
2 tsp. baking powder
1 Tbsp. sugar
½ tsp. salt
3 Tbsp. butter or margarine, softened
1 cup buttermilk or soured milk
Bench flour (to flour your work surface or for extra-sticky dough)
¼ cup raisins (optional)
¼ cup currants (optional)
2 tsp. caraway seeds (optional)

Preheat oven to 350°. Sift together flour, baking soda, baking powder, sugar and salt. Cut in butter or margarine. Add remaining ingredients and mix thoroughly. Turn out on floured board (this is when you use your bench flour) and knead for 2 to 3 minutes.

Place rounded loaf in a greased 9-inch pie pan and spread to an even level. Cut a cross on the top with a sharp, floured knife. Bake for 30 to 45 minutes, checking after 25 minutes, or until golden brown on top. Serve warm with butter and best eaten the same day.

Dough is approximately the same as biscuits or scones. Make sour milk by putting 1 tablespoon vinegar into regular milk and let sit a few minutes.

Claudia Finnegan

PINEAPPLE TURNOVERS

This is also good with blueberry or apple pie filling.

6 cups flour
1 cake or pkg. yeast
1 lb. lard
3 eggs
1 tsp. salt
¾ cup milk
1 tsp. sugar
1 can crushed pineapple
1 cup sugar
1½ Tbsp. cornstarch

Work flour, yeast and lard as for pie dough. Beat eggs and add milk. Add to flour mixture and mix well. Chill overnight. Work with small pieces of dough, leaving the rest chilled. Roll out about 1.8 inch thick. Cut into 3 x 3-inch squares or rounds.

Cook pineapple, sugar and cornstarch until thickened. Chill overnight for easier handling.

Place 1 teaspoon filling in center of each piece of dough. Fold to form triangle, sealing edges with fork tines. Roll in granulated sugar. Bake on greased baking sheet at 350° for about 20 minutes or until brown.

.

Paddy Gerbic

POTECA

Poteca is a Yugoslavian/Romanian bread that we had only at Christmas and how we waited all year for our first taste!

BREAD
1- 3 oz. pkg. dry yeast
¼ cup warm water.
½ cup + 2 Tbsp. buttermilk
1 egg
¼ cup butter
¼ cup sugar
1 tsp. baking powder
1 tsp. salt
2½-3 cups flour

Dissolve yeast in water, then mix with buttermilk, egg, butter, sugar baking powder and salt and 1 cup of flour. Beat 2 minutes on medium with mixer. Add remaining flour to make dough easy to handle.

Turn dough out on floured board. Knead. Roll out to a 24 x 15-inch rectangle. Dough will be very thin.

FILLING
2 cups walnuts, chopped
½ cup brown sugar
¼ cup butter, softened
¼ cup milk
1 egg
½ tsp. vanilla extract
½ tsp. lemon extract

Spread filling to cover dough. Roll up as a jellyroll. Place on greased baking sheet. Let rise until double in volume.
Bake at 375° for 30 to 35 minutes. Brush with butter while hot.

Dorothe Cavanaugh

STIR AND BAKE ROLLS

2 cups warm (not hot) water
1 pkg. yeast
¼ cup of sugar
1 egg
¾ cup oil
4 cups self-rising flour

Pour water into large mixing bowl with lid. Add yeast and sugar. Stir well. Add egg and oil and then stir in flour. Let set out 10 to 15 minutes then cover and refrigerate. When ready to bake, stir dough down, half fill greased muffin tins and bake at 450° till brown. Dough keeps for one week.

If you do not have self rising flour, you may substitute with all-purpose flour or a combination of all-purpose flour and whole wheat flour 1½ cup but must add 4 teaspoons baking powder and 2 teaspoons salt to the total of 4 cups of flour.

You may also substitute the white sugar with brown sugar and if you prefer a sweeter roll, may increase the sugar from ¼ cup to ¾ cup.

Jayne Martin

ST. PHILIP MEN'S CLUB ST. VALENTINE'S DAY BREAKFAST FOR THE LADIES BISCUITS

2 cups Martha White self-rising flour
1 tsp. baking powder
⅛ tsp. baking soda
Dash salt
1 cup buttermilk (not low fat)
¼ lb. butter

Preheat oven to 450°. Sift dry ingredients, making sure they are well mixed. Cut in butter until the consistency of coarse crumbs. Make a well and pour in buttermilk all at once. Stir quickly with fork just until thoroughly mixed. Turn onto heavily floured surface. Knead gently about one minute. Pat or roll dough to about ½ to ¾ inch thick. Cut with biscuit cutter. Place on greased cookie sheet with sides touching. Place in oven on middle rack for 10 minutes.

Remove from oven and separate biscuits, return for 5 more minutes or until tops are brown and sides are done.

Vic Sancricca

Brunch

BENEDICTINE SANDWICHES

This recipe is out of Louisville, Kentucky. It is a must for all Derby parties and ladies' luncheons in the Louisville area. Sometimes it is served as a dip with toast points.

1 medium cucumber
1 small onion quartered
1- 8-oz. package cream cheese, softened
½ tsp. salt
Dash hot pepper sauce
1 drop green food coloring
Thinly sliced white bread
Mayonnaise
Parsley or watercress, for garnish (optional)

Peel cucumber and slice in half lengthwise; remove seeds with a small spoon. Place cucumber in a food processor and pulse about 5 times, until cucumber is minced. Place cucumber into a small glass mixing bowl. Place onion in the food processor, pulsing until it is finely chopped. Add onion to cucumber. Add cream cheese and stir well with a spatula. Add salt, hot sauce, and food coloring.

Cut the crust off bread slices and cut each slice in half, or with a round cookie or biscuit cutter, cut rounds out of bread slices. Spread a small amount of mayonnaise on bread slices/rounds. Spread cheese mixture on half the slice/rounds and top with another slice/round. Garnish with a sprig of parsley or watercress.

Nena Manci

CRANBERRY APPLE CASSEROLE

Great for a brunch!

3 cups apples, chopped
2 cups fresh cranberries (I use entire package of berries)
3 Tbsp. flour
1 cup sugar
3 pkg. instant oatmeal with cinnamon apple spice
¾ cup pecans, chopped (bake 5 minutes to release flavor)
½ cup flour
½ cup brown sugar
½ cup butter, melted

Combine apples, cranberries and flour, tossing to coat fruit. Add 1 cup sugar and mix well. Place in 2-quart casserole.
Combine oatmeal, pecans, ½ cup flour and ½ cup brown sugar. Add melted butter and mix well. Spoon over fruit. Bake uncovered at 350° for 45 minutes.

Mary Ann Thompson

EGG AND HAM BRUNCH

½ pkg. frozen broccoli florets
2 cups ham, diced
1½ cups Cheddar cheese, shredded
1 cup Bisquick
3 cups milk
4 eggs

Preheat oven to 350°. Spray 9 x 13-inch pan and set aside. Cook broccoli and drain; spread broccoli in the bottom of the pan and layer ham and cheese over broccoli. Beat together eggs, milk and Bisquick. Pour over broccoli, ham and cheese in pan. Bake 55 minutes to one hour, uncovered. Let sit about 5 minutes and then cut into portions and serve.

Patty Story

OVERNIGHT CARAMEL FRENCH TOAST

1 cup brown sugar, firmly packed
1 stick unsalted butter
2 Tbsp. light corn syrup
12 slices Pepperidge Farm sliced French bread (no ends)
¼ cup granulated sugar
1 teaspoon ground cinnamon
6 large eggs, beaten
1½ cups half-and-half cream
1 tsp. vanilla extract
¼ tsp. salt
1 cup pecans, toasted
Whipped cream

Lightly butter a 13 x 9- inch baking dish; set aside. In a medium saucepan, bring brown sugar, butter and corn syrup to a boil. Remove from heat and pour into prepared baking dish. Put 12 slices of bread over caramel mixture in pan. In a small bowl, combine sugar and cinnamon; sprinkle over bread in pan. In a large mixing bowl, beat eggs, cream, vanilla and salt; pour over bread in pan. Cover and refrigerate overnight.
Remove dish from refrigerator. Preheat oven to 350°. Bake French toast 30 to 35 minutes, or until lightly browned. Serve with toasted pecans and whipped cream for garnish.

Jeanette Teague

NIGHT BEFORE FRENCH TOAST

1 loaf of French bread, ¾ inch slices
4 Tbsp. butter, melted
2/3 cup brown sugar
1 tsp. cinnamon
4 eggs
2 cups milk

Melt butter and mix brown sugar in a 9 x 13-inch dish. Lay bread on top of mixture. Combine eggs, milk and cinnamon. Pour over bread. Cover and refrigerate overnight. Bake at 350° for 45 minutes.

Jayne Martin

FRENCH TOAST CASSEROLE

8 slices cinnamon swirl bread
8 oz. cream cheese, softened
¼ cup sugar
4 eggs
½ cup milk
1 ½ tsp. cinnamon

Beat together cream cheese and sugar and spread generously on each slice of bread and sandwich together. In a greased, 8 inch-square baking dish, place each of the 4 "sandwiches" to cover pan. Whisk together the eggs, milk and cinnamon. Pour egg mixture over bread and refrigerate overnight. Bake at 350 ° for 30 to 35 minutes.

Jenny Turner

HAM AND CHEESE CASSEROLE

2 Tbsp. margarine
½ cup onion, chopped
½ cup green pepper, chopped
1 can cream of celery soup
8 oz. sour cream
8 oz. fettuccine, cooked and drained
2 cups ham, cubed
1-2 cups Swiss cheese, shredded

Sauté onions and green peppers in margarine. Combine with celery soup and sour cream. In a large bowl, combine fettuccine, ham, cheese and soup mixture. Add an additional ¼ cup of milk if mixture appears too dry. Transfer to a greased 13 x 9- baking dish and bake at 350°for 30 to 45 minutes.

Jenny Turner

KENTUCKY HOT BROWN CASSEROLE

8 slices bread, toasted and cubed
1 lb. turkey, cubed
1 cup butter
1 cup all-purpose flour
4 cups milk
1 lb. cheddar cheese, shredded
½ cup grated Parmesan cheese
1 lb. bacon, cooked and crumbled
1 medium tomato, seeded and diced

Preheat oven to 350°. Lightly grease a 13 x 9-inch baking dish. Place toasted bread evenly over bottom of prepared baking dish. Layer ham and turkey evenly over bread. In a large skillet, melt butter over medium heat. Whisk in flour until smooth; cook 2 minutes, whisking constantly. Gradually whisk in milk; cook 3 to 4 minutes, whisking constantly, or until thickened. Add cheeses, stirring until melted and smooth. Pour over turkey. Sprinkle evenly with bacon and tomato. Bake 20 to 25 minutes, or until hot and bubbly.

Nena Manci

LOUISVILLE GARLIC CHEESE GRITS

4½ cups boiling water
1 tsp. salt
1 cup quick grits
2 eggs
2/3 cup milk
½ stick butter
2 tsp. garlic powder

Boil softly grits and salt in water for 15 to 20 minutes, then add butter and garlic powder. Beat 2 eggs and add 2/3 cup milk to make 1 cup liquid. Stir into grits mixture. Place in Pam-sprayed 2 quart casserole. Bake at 350° for 1½ hours.

Carole Guthrie

FR. KIRK'S OATMEAL BREAKFAST

½ cup old-fashioned oats
¼ cup water
8 oz. orange juice
½ glass milk
2 pieces wheat bread
Honey

Pour the water into the oats and place in microwave for 3 minutes.
Place the bread into the toaster.
Take the oats out of the microwave and pour milk in.
Take bread out of the toaster and top with honey.
Drink the orange juice.

Father John Kirk

Enjoy one of these four great quiche recipes for brunch, lunch or for a light evening meal. Spinach quiche is a good Lenten choice.

QUICHE

1 pie crust
4 eggs (5 for deep dish)
2 cups sharp Cheddar and Swiss cheese, grated
1 cup half & half
1 cup bacon, ham or sausage, cooked
Salt and pepper to taste

Place pie crust in pie plate. Place cooked meat on bottom, cover with cheese. Beat eggs, add milk and seasoning, then pour into crust. Bake at 350° for 45 minutes or until solid.
Can be done ahead and reheated. Can also be frozen and reheated. You can also add vegetables like asparagus to this.

Jeannette Teague

SPINACH QUICHE

1 frozen prepared pie shell
3 Tbsp. extra virgin olive oil
1 cup onion, chopped
2- 4 oz. jars chopped pimentos, excess liquid squeezed out
3 garlic cloves, minced
1- 10 oz. pkg. frozen leaf spinach, thawed, excess liquid squeezed out and chopped
3 large eggs
¼ cup Parmesan cheese, grated
1 cup milk
2/3 cup crumbled feta

Preheat oven to 375°. Blind bake the crust by lining the pie shell with aluminum foil and weighting it down with pie weights or beans. Bake for 15 to 20 minutes until light golden brown. Increase oven temperature to 375°.

In a large skillet, heat oil over moderate heat. Add onion and cook until softened. Turn up heat to moderately high. Add pimentos, garlic and spinach and cook, stirring until just heated through. Drain off any excess liquid.

Beat the eggs in a bowl and add the Parmesan cheese and milk. Add the spinach mixture and feta, and pour into the pie shell. Bake on a sheet pan in the middle of the oven for 30 to 35 minutes or until just set.

Kay Dozier

QUICHE LORRAINE

1 prepared pie crust
1 cup Swiss cheese, shredded
12 slices of bacon, fried and crumbled
⅓ cup onion, minced
2 cups whipping or light cream
⅛ tsp. red pepper
¾ tsp. salt
¼ tsp. sugar
4 eggs

Preheat oven to 425°. Sprinkle bacon, cheese, and onion into pie crust. Slightly beat eggs; beat in the remaining ingredients then pour cream mixture into pie crust. Bake for 15 minutes. Bake for 30 minutes longer at 300° or until knife comes clean inserted 1 inch from edge. Before cutting let stand 10 minutes. Serve in wedges.

Carol McNally

HASHBROWN QUICHE

2-3 large fresh potatoes, finely diced
2 Tbsp. water
4 Tbsp. butter, melted
4-5 eggs, beaten
¾ cup of milk
1 cup ham, diced
1 cup fresh spinach, chopped
Salt and pepper

Preheat oven to 450°. Steam potatoes with water in the microwave for about 3 to 4 minutes. Pour butter on steamed potatoes, toss and then mash into the bottom of a greased pie pan. Put in preheated oven for 25 minutes. While potato crust is baking, in a bowl, mix beaten eggs, milk, ham, spinach, shredded cheese, salt and pepper. After crust comes out of oven, pour mixture over cooked hashbrown crust. Lower oven temperature to 350° and cook another 20 minutes.

Holly Moore

SAUSAGE CRESCENT ROLLS

24-30 crescent rolls
16 oz. regular sausage
8 oz. hot sausage
1 onion, chopped fine
14 oz. sauerkraut, drained and chopped fine
3 oz. cream cheese, softened
1 tsp. dry mustard
¼ tsp. garlic powder
Dash salt and pepper
1 Tbsp. parsley

Brown and drain sausage and onion. Set aside. Mix remaining ingredients, then add meat mixture. Mix well and chill for 1 hour. Spread out crescent rolls and place a spoonful of meat in center. Tuck sides and roll. Bake at 375° for 12 to 15 minutes until golden brown.

Phyllis Hesse

SUNRISE CASSEROLE

2- 12 oz. pkgs. breakfast sausage links
9 large eggs
3 cups milk
1½ tsp. ground mustard
1 tsp. salt
½ tsp. pepper
2- 20 oz. pkgs. refrigerated hash browns
2 cups Cheddar cheese, shredded
½ cup sweet red pepper, diced (optional)
⅓ cup green onion, thinly sliced
Salsa or picante sauce (optional)

Bake sausage in oven 15-20 minutes until no longer pink; drain. Slice into ¼ inch coins. In large bowl combine eggs, milk, mustard and green onions. Mix well. Place in pan over sausage. Cover and refrigerate overnight. Remove 30 minutes before baking. Bake uncovered at 350° for 65 to 70 minutes until set and golden brown. Let stand 10 minutes and serve with salsa or picante sauce if desired.

Jackie Ellis

Soups

CHEESY BAKED POTATO SOUP

32 oz. pkg. shredded hash brown potatoes
½ cup yellow onion, chopped
½ cup green onion, chopped, plus extra for topping
¼ cup celery, diced
¼ cup carrots, diced (optional)
32 oz. chicken broth
1 cup water
1½ tsp. kosher salt
1 tsp. ground pepper
3 Tbsp. all-purpose flour
1 cup heavy cream
2 cups sharp cheddar cheese, shredded (plus extra for topping)
¼ cup crisp bacon bits, crumbled
¼ cup fresh chives, chopped
Cracked pepper for topping (optional)
Sour cream for topping (optional)

In a 3 to 4-quart crock pot add water, broth, onions, green onions, carrots, salt, pepper and potatoes. Cook on low setting for 6 to 8 hours until potatoes are tender. Add flour to heavy cream and stir until smooth. Add cream mixture to crock pot and cook on high for 20 to 30 minutes or until mixture is thickened. Add Cheddar cheese and stir until melted. Cook on low for 10 to 15 minutes then turn to "keep warm" setting. When ready to serve, sprinkle bacon, fchive, pepper, and a little green onion over each bowl of soup and serve warm.

Holly Moore
Lindsey Garansuay

CHICKEN TACO SOUP

A lot of cans for recycling but very easy.

1-1½ lbs. chicken breasts
6 cups chicken broth
1 onion, chopped
1 green pepper, chopped
1 tsp. garlic salt

Cook the chicken breasts in the broth with the onion, garlic salt and pepper.

Remove chicken to cool, once cooled shred into pieces. As chicken cools add back to broth.

MIX
1-15 oz. can diced tomatoes
1-10 oz. can Rotel tomatoes with chilies
1 garlic clove, minced
1-15 oz. can small pinto beans (not drained)
1-15 oz. can black beans, drained
1-15 oz. can cream corn
1-15 oz. can regular kernel corn, shoepeg, or whatever
1 pkg. Old El Paso taco seasoning mix
⅓ pkg. ranch dressing mix
½ tsp. cumin

Add chicken and broth. Stir and simmer 30 minutes.

Soup is better served the next day, and served with tortilla chips and shredded cheddar cheese

Jean Berry

CHICKEN TORTILLA SOUP

1½ lb. chicken, cooked and shredded (I use pressure cooker because the chicken shreds better)
1-15 oz. can whole tomatoes
10 oz. enchilada sauce
1 medium onion, chopped
1- 4 oz. can green chilies, chopped
1 clove garlic, minced
2 cups water (I use water that I cooked chicken in)
1- 14 oz. can chicken broth
1 tsp. cumin
1 tsp. chili powder
1 tsp. salt
¼ tsp. black pepper
1 bay leaf
1-10 oz. pkg. frozen corn
1 Tbsp. cilantro

Place all ingredients in crock pot on low for 8 hours. Or can be ready to serve after simmering as long as you can stand it! Can heat and eat when in a hurry. Serve with tortilla chips.

Cory McCormick

CORN AND CHICKEN SOUP

3-4 lb. chicken
1 lb. egg noodles
1 rib celery
1 pkg. frozen corn
6 potatoes, peeled and diced
Parsley flakes
Salt and pepper to taste

Boil the chicken, celery, and parsley for 2 hours. Cool the chicken and remove it from the bone. Add the remaining items and simmer until the potatoes are tender.

Ruth Ann Graveno

CREAM OF BROCCOLI SOUP

1½ quarts water (6 cups)
1-10 oz. pkg. frozen chopped broccoli
¾ cup finely chopped onion
2 tsp. salt
2 tsp. MSG (optional)
1 tsp. white pepper
1 tsp. garlic powder
8 oz. sharp cheese, shredded
1 cup milk
1 cup cream
¼ cup butter
⅓ cup flour
½ cup cold water

In 3-quart saucepan, bring water to boil. Add broccoli and onion and boil for 10 to12 minutes. Add seasonings and shredded cheese. Stir until cheese melts. Add milk, cream and butter; stir and heat to boiling. Slowly add cold water to flour, stirring constantly until texture is smooth. Slowly add to hot mixture, stirring rapidly. Cook and stir until soup is consistency of heavy cream.

Carole Guthrie

RED BEAN SOUP

2 cans red beans, preferable Blue Runner, but any creamy brand will do
2 cans beef broth
1 can mild Rotel tomatoes, with green chilies
1 cup onion, chopped
1 cup celery, chopped
1 cup carrots, sliced

Stir together beans, broth and tomatoes. Then add onion, celery and carrots. Sliced sausage may be added.

Judy Tujague

CREAMY SOUTHWESTERN PUMPKIN SOUP

2 Tbsp. butter or olive oil
1 onion, chopped
1 jalapeno pepper, chopped
2 garlic cloves, minced (I use a lot more, like 5 cloves....we love garlic)
5 cups chicken broth (I use 2 cans of vegetable broth)
1 medium potato, chopped and peeled
1¼ tsp salt
½ tsp. chili powder
½ tsp. cumin
1-15 oz. can pumpkin puree
2 cups milk, half and half or combination of the two
Lime juice

Sauté onion, jalapeno and garlic in butter or oil for about 15 minutes. Add broth and next 5 ingredients. Cook, stirring often, for about 30 minutes or until potato is tender. Smooth out with a hand blender or in batches in blender or food processor. Stir in milk or half and half and simmer for about 10 minutes. Serve with a squeeze of fresh lime juice on top. You can also garnish with fresh chopped cilantro and sour cream.

Holly Moore

GAZPACHO

3 tomatoes, diced
1 green pepper, diced
1 cucumber, peeled and diced
3 green onions, diced

1 lg. jar V-8 juice
3 garlic cloves, minced
2 Tbsp. olive oil
2 Tbsp. red wine vinegar
Salt and pepper to taste

Combine all ingredients. Chill and serve.

Margie Thessin

HEARTY ITALIAN SOUP

1-16 oz. pkg. Italian sausage
2 tsp. olive oil
1 lg. onion, diced
2 garlic cloves, minced
1- 48 oz. container chicken broth
2- 15 oz. cans cannellini beans
2 -14½ oz. cans diced tomatoes
1 tsp. dried Italian seasoning
1- 5 oz. pkg. baby spinach
¼ cup fresh parsley, chopped
¼ cup fresh basil, chopped
Parmesan cheese, freshly shaved

Cook sausage in hot oil in a Dutch oven over medium heat 7 to 8 minutes or until browned. Remove sausage and reserve drippings.

Sauté onion in drippings 3 minutes or until tender. Add garlic and sauté 1 minute. Cut sausage into ¼ inch slices and return to pot. Stir chicken broth and next 3 ingredients into sausage mixture.

Bring to boil over medium high heat. Reduce heat to medium-low and simmer 25 minutes.

Stir in spinach and next 2 ingredients. Cook for 5 to 6 minutes until spinach is wilted. Serve with Parmesan cheese.

Terry Bies

MEATLESS CHILI

I have this every Ash Wednesday.

1 Tbsp. olive oil
1 large onion, chopped
2 large tomatoes, chopped or 1-14 ½ oz. can chopped tomatoes
1- 4 oz. can chopped green chilies, undrained
1 tsp. ground cumin
1 Tbsp. chili powder
1-15 oz. can red kidney beans, undrained
1-15 oz. can great northern beans, undrained
¼ tsp. cilantro leaves, chopped (optional)

Heat oil in large saucepan over medium heat. Add onion; cook until tender, stirring occasionally. Stir in tomatoes, chilies with liquid, chili powder and cumin. Bring to a boil. Add beans with liquid. Reduce heat to low; cover. Simmer 15 minutes, stirring occasionally.

Sprinkle individual servings with cilantro and shredded cheddar cheese.

Jean Berry

SOPA DE TORTILLA

1- 8 oz. can tomatoes
1 medium onion, cut up
1 clove garlic
2 Tbsp snipped cilantro or parsley
¼ tsp sugar
4 cups chicken or vegetable broth
6 corn tortillas*
Cooking oil
1 cup shredded Monterey Jack or 4 oz. longhorn cheese

In blender container combine undrained tomatoes, onion, garlic, cilantro and sugar. Cover and blend till nearly smooth. Turn into a large saucepan; stir in broth. Bring to boil, cover and simmer for 20 minutes.

Meanwhile cut tortillas into ½-inch wide strips. Fry strips in ½ inch hot oil for 40 to 60 seconds or till crisp and lightly browned. Drain on paper towel.

Divide fried tortilla strips and cheese among soup bowls. Ladle soup over, serve immediately.

If desired top with fresh cilantro and/or avocado. *May use unsalted tortilla chips or strips.

Ana Anaya

POT LIQUOR SOUP

Sometimes spelled Pot Likker, this soup is a traditional Southern New Year's Day dish.

2 lbs. fresh collard greens, torn in bite-sized pieces and large tough stems removed along with any discoloration or damage.
2 lbs. ham pieces, cut in bite-sized pieces
2 Tbsp. hot sauce
3 Tbsp. olive oil
2 large onions, chopped
1 garlic clove, minced
10 red potatoes, diced
4 cups strong chicken stock
2-16 oz. cans field peas, drained
2-16 oz. cans crowder peas, drained
2 cups water
½ cup vermouth
1 Tbsp. white vinegar
1 tsp. salt

In a large pot cover collard greens with water and bring to a boil. Remove from heat and drain. In a bowl toss together ham pieces and hot sauce. Put olive oil in a skillet until hot and sauté ham pieces and hot sauce over medium-high heat until browned. Add onion and garlic and sauté until tender. Add to collard greens with potatoes and remaining ingredients. Bring to a boil, reduce heat and simmer 45 minutes, stirring occasionally.

Gwen Perkins, Chapman's II

SAUSAGE-TORTELLINI SOUP

This is a wonderful and healthy soup!

1 lb. Italian sausage
1 large onion, chopped
3 garlic cloves, minced
3-14½ oz. cans beef broth
3-14½ oz. cans diced tomatoes, undrained
1- 8 oz. can tomato sauce
1 cup dry red wine or 1 cup dark beer
½ tsp. fennel
4 carrots, thinly sliced
1 Tbsp. sugar
2 tsp. Italian seasoning
3 small zucchini, sliced
1- 9 oz. pkg. refrigerated cheese-filled tortellini
1 cup Parmesan cheese, shredded

Discard sausage casings. Cook sausage, onion, and garlic in soup pot on medium heat, stirring until sausage crumbles and is no longer pink. Drain. Return mixture to pan. Stir in broth and next 7 ingredients. Bring to boil. Reduce heat simmer and 30 minutes. Skim off fat. Stir in zucchini and tortellini and simmer 10 minutes.

Sprinkle each serving with cheese.

Kay Dozier

VEGETABLE AND MEATBALL SOUP

6 cups water
4 cups canned diced tomatoes
1½ cup celery, chopped
2 cups carrots, sliced
1 large onion, sliced
4 tsp. salt
2 bay leaves
2 Tbsp. parsley, chopped
2 tsp. seasoned pepper
2 tsp. ground basil
1 lb. ground beef
1 egg
¼ cup cracker crumbs
1 Tbsp. milk
1 tsp. salt
¼ tsp. pepper
1 pkg. frozen mixed vegetables

Combine water through basil in a large Dutch oven, cover and bring to a boil. Combine ground beef, egg, cracker crumbs, milk, salt and pepper, mix well with hands. Shape meat mixture into 1 inch balls.

Drop meatballs into boiling soup. Simmer for 30 minutes. Add vegetables. Cook another 10 to 15 minutes.

Variations include adding either potatoes, peeled and diced before adding meatballs, or partially cooked pastina. Serve with Parmesan cheese.

Louise Volpe

WEDDING SOUP

4-5 large cans chicken broth (College Inn)
4-5 baked boneless chicken breasts, cut in cubes
1 large bag of greens (or 2-3 boxes frozen spinach thawed and drained well)
Medium bag of very small meatballs (can find this at an Italian store)
Celery cut in small pieces to taste
4-6 eggs, scrambled but not cooked
Romano cheese, grated, to taste

In stock pot mix all ingredients except eggs and cheese. Simmer 1 hour. Pour raw scrambled eggs slowly into soup while stirring. Eggs will then cook. Add cheese to taste. Mix. Simmer 15 minutes.

Bunnie McCormick

WHITE CHICKEN CHILI

1 can cream of chicken soup
6 cups chicken broth
1 onion, chopped
2 cloves garlic, chopped
2 cans green chilies, chopped
1 large jar or 3 cans great northern beans
½ Tbsp. oregano
½ Tbsp. tarragon
1 Tbsp. cumin
Pinch red pepper
½ tsp. salt
½ tsp. black pepper
4 cups chicken, cooked and shredded
8 oz. Monterey Jack cheese, shredded
Sour cream to taste

Combine all ingredients except chicken and simmer for 1 hour. Add chicken and simmer 15 minutes longer. Top with the cheese and sour cream.

Ashley Blackburn

WHITE BEAN CHICKEN CHILI

1 or 2 onions, chopped
1 cup sweet red peppers, chopped
2 Tbsp. vegetable oil
3 boneless skinless chicken breasts, cooked and chopped
2-16-oz. cans great northern beans
2-16 oz. cans chicken broth
1-10 oz. package frozen white corn
1- 4 oz. can diced green chilies
1 cup fresh parsley, chopped
1 tsp. white pepper
1 tsp. ground cumin
1 tsp. salt
Coriander to taste
Tortilla strips

Sauté the onion and peppers in the oil in a Dutch oven until tender. Add the chicken, undrained beans, broth, corn, green chilies, parsley, white pepper, cumin, salt and coriander and mix well. Simmer over low heat for 1 hour or until desired consistency, stirring occasionally. Ladle into chili bowls and garnish with tortilla strips.

Marilyn DiNardo

YUMMY CROCK POT BAKED POTATO SOUP

5 lbs. russet potatoes, washed but not peeled, diced into ½-inch cubes
1 medium to large yellow onion, diced
10 cloves of garlic, minced (or 5 tsp. jarred minced garlic)
8 cups chicken stock or broth
16 oz. cream cheese, softened (I use low fat)
1 Tbsp. seasoned salt
Optional garnishes: crumbled bacon, shredded cheese, green onions

Add potatoes, onion, garlic, seasoning, and chicken stock to slow cooker. Cook on high for 6 hours or low for 10 hours.

Add the softened cream cheese and puree soup with an immersion blender until the cheese is incorporated and about half the soup is blended. Alternately you could remove half the soup and the cream cheese to an upright blender, then re-incorporate.

Stir well, top with your choice of garnishes and enjoy!

Mary Grindstaff

Salads

BEEF ASPARAGUS SALAD

This is best made ahead. It is great for luncheons or picnics.

⅓ cup light soy sauce
¼ cup rice wine vinegar
1½ in. piece fresh ginger, peeled and grated
1 tsp. sugar
White pepper to taste
4 cups (about 2 pounds) fresh asparagus, diagonally cut into 1½ inch pieces
2 cups broccoli, cut into florets
1½ lb. flank steak, grilled to medium-rare (cook ahead and cool)
1 red bell pepper, cut into bite-size pieces

In a medium bowl, mix soy sauce, vinegar, ginger, sugar and white pepper. Slice grilled steak into bite-sized pieces and toss with dressing. Allow to stand several hours or overnight in refrigerator. Bring a large pot of water to a boil. Drop in asparagus spears and blanch 30 seconds. Drain with a slotted spoon and cool in a colander under running water. Add broccoli to same water, blanch for 30 seconds, remove and cool as asparagus. Add vegetables to steak and dressing shortly before serving and toss again. Serve at room temperature.

Nancy Tuberty

CHICKEN PASTA SALAD

16 oz. pasta cooked (I like bowtie for this recipe)
1½ cup red grapes
1½ cup green grapes
¼ cup white vinegar
¼ cup pineapple juice
2 cups mayonnaise
1 cup sour cream
1-15 oz. can Mandarin oranges
1-15 oz. can pineapple tidbits
3 cups chicken, cooked and diced
¾ cup sugar

Combine vinegar, pineapple juice, mayonnaise, sour cream and sugar to make dressing. Pour over rest of ingredients to combine. Serve and enjoy! May be made ahead and refrigerated for several days.

Holly Moore

CHICKEN SALAD WITH ARTICHOKES

4 chicken breast halves, cooked and cubed
1-14 oz. can artichoke hearts, drained and chopped
¾ cup mayonnaise
¾ cup celery, chopped
6 green onions, chopped
1 cup, pecans, chopped
¼ tsp. salt
⅛ tsp. garlic salt
⅛ tsp. pepper
Sandwich bread or lettuce leaves

Combine. Refrigerate until serving time.

Jackie Ellis

CHICKEN TORTELLINI PASTA SALAD

This pasta salad is great for potlucks. Every time I make it I get asked to share the recipe.

6 skinless chicken breasts, cooked and cut into strips
2 Tbsp. olive oil
2 garlic gloves, minced
¾ cup cider vinegar
¼ cup honey
1 Tbsp. fresh basil, chopped or 1 tsp. dried basil
3 Tbsp. fresh parsley, chopped
2 tsp. Dijon mustard
1 tsp. dry mustard
¾ cup vegetable oil
1 red pepper, seeded and chopped
1 green pepper, seeded and chopped
3 ribs celery, sliced
1 red onion, chopped
Salt and pepper to taste
10 oz. fresh tortellini
Fresh Parmesan cheese to top

The night before, cook chicken and cut into strips. Heat olive oil in large skillet and add garlic. Sauté over medium heat until golden brown then add cooked chicken. Sauté 1 minute, stirring constantly. Remove garlic and chicken to large bowl. Set aside.

In a small bowl combine vinegar, honey, basil, parsley and dry and Dijon mustards. Whisk in the vegetable oil, blending until creamy. Pour dressing over garlic and chicken. Cover and marinate overnight.

Before serving, cook tortellini then drain and cool. To assemble salad combine marinated chicken with dressing, tortellini, chopped peppers, celery, onion, salt and pepper. Toss well and serve with fresh Parmesan cheese.

Stephanie Carroll

CRAB AND ARTICHOKE ORZO SALAD

1 lb. orzo
1- 6 oz. jar marinated artichoke heart quarters, drained, 4 reserved and the rest coarsely chopped
2 garlic cloves
1 shallot, chopped
1 tsp. Dijon mustard
1 tsp. Greek oregano
2 large basil leaves
½ cup white wine vinegar
¾ cup extra virgin olive oil
Salt and freshly ground pepper
10 oil packed sun-dried tomato halves, drained and sliced into ¼ inch strips
5 scallions, thinly sliced crosswise
1 lb. jumbo lump crabmeat picked over
2 Tbsp. parsley, chopped

Cook orzo until al dente. Drain and rinse under cold water. Meanwhile, in a blender, puree the four reserved artichokes with the garlic, shallot, mustard, oregano, basil and vinegar. With the blender on, pour in olive oil. Season with salt and pepper. Stir 1 cup of the vinaigrette into the orzo. Add the chopped artichokes, sun-dried tomatoes, scallions, crabmeat and parsley. Serve in bowls passing the remaining vinaigrette at the table.

Terry Bies

ELEVEN LAYER SALAD

1st layer: lettuce, chopped
2nd layer: celery, chopped
3rd layer: green onion, chopped
4th layer: green pepper, chopped
5th layer: frozen peas, thawed but not cooked
6th layer: thin layer mayonnaise
7th layer: 2 Tbsp. sugar
8th layer: 1 cup cheddar cheese, grated
9th layer: 1 cup mozzarella cheese, grated
10th layer: 8 pieces fried bacon, crumbled
11th layer: Parmesan cheese

Cover and refrigerate overnight.

Cory McCormick

Fruit salad is a healthful addition to any meal. Here are two yummy ones!

FRUIT SALAD I

½ cup sugar
2 Tbsp. cornstarch
¾ cup pineapple juice
½ cup orange juice
1 Tbsp. lemon juice
2 cans pineapple tidbits, drained, reserve juice
2 cans Mandarin oranges, drained
1 red apple, chopped
2 green apples, chopped

Heat sugar, cornstarch and juices on stove and pour over fruit while it is still hot. Store uncovered in refrigerator for 24 hours
May add banana before serving. This is good for a couple days.

Jackie Ellis

FRUIT SALAD II

1-15 oz. can whole berry cranberry sauce
1-15 oz. can crushed pineapple, drained
1-15 oz. can mandarin oranges, drained
1 cup pecans or walnuts, chopped

Mix and refrigerate in sealable bowl.

Jayne Martin

GARDEN SALAD

1¼ cup sugar
¾ cup oil
¾ cup vinegar
1¼ tsp. pepper
1 cup bell pepper, chopped
2 bunches green onion, chopped
1 cup celery, chopped
1 can shoe peg corn
1 can French-cut green beans
1 can small sweet peas
1 large jar sliced pimento

Boil sugar, oil, vinegar and pepper in small pan until sugar is dissolved. Allow to cool. Drain cans of vegetables and mix with remaining ingredients. Pour cooled dressing over vegetables. Refrigerate overnight. Keeps for two weeks.

Sherri Witherall

HONEY MUSTARD SALAD DRESSING

¼ cup vinegar
¼ cup pureed onion or 2 Tbsp. dried minced onion
¼ cup sugar
1 cup honey
6 oz. Gulden's brown mustard
1½ cups mayonnaise
1 cup buttermilk

Mix together and refrigerate.

Nancy Tuberty

ITALIAN PASTA SALAD
This tasty salad is pictured on the book's cover

3 cups penne pasta, cooked, drained (8 oz. uncooked)
1 cup broccoli florets
½ cup red pepper, sliced
½ cup green pepper, sliced
½ cup red onion, sliced
½ tsp. oregano
Salt and pepper to taste
1 cup Italian dressing or Caesar dressing
½ cup pitted black olives (optional)
½ cup Parmesan cheese, grated (optional)

Toss all ingredients except dressing in large bowl. Add dressing and mix lightly. Refrigerate several hours or overnight before serving.

Jeanette Teague

HONEY POPPY SEED PASTA SALAD

1 lb. wagon wheel pasta
1 rotisserie chicken (I get mine at Sam's)
1 yellow pepper, chopped
1 orange pepper, chopped
1 cup snow pea pods, halved lengthwise
1 apple, cored and diced (use a bit of lemon to keep it from browning)
1 cup grapes, halved
3 scallions, thinly sliced
½ cup mayonnaise (I use light Miracle Whip)
¼ cup honey
3 Tbsp. cider vinegar
2 Tbsp. Dijon mustard
Zest of ½ orange
1 Tbsp. poppy seeds
½ tsp. salt
¼ tsp. ground black pepper
½ cup toasted slivered almonds (optional)

Cook pasta in large pot according to directions, drain and then transfer to a paper or kitchen towel lined baking sheet to cool and dry. Meanwhile remove meat from chicken and shred or chop. Mix chicken, veggies and fruit in a large bowl. In a small bowl, whisk together the mayonnaise, honey, vinegar, mustard, orange zest, poppy seeds, salt and pepper. When the pasta is cooled add to chicken mixture, toss and combine. Pour dressing over chicken mixture and stir to coat. Sprinkle with almonds. This can be prepared well in advance.

Mary Ann Thompson

HONEY-GINGER VINAIGRETTE

1- 1½ inch piece fresh ginger, peeled
1 garlic clove
2 Tbsp. rice wine vinegar
1 Tbsp. soy sauce
1 Tbsp. honey
⅛ tsp. dried crushed red pepper
¼ cup peanut oil
½ tsp. dark sesame oil

Process ginger and garlic in food processor until smooth. Add vinegar and next 3 ingredients. Process 30 seconds and then slowly pour peanut oil and sesame oil into mixture on low until smooth.

Gwen Perkins, Chapman's II

JOANNE'S BROCCOLI SALAD

1 pkg. Oriental-flavor Ramen noodles
1½ pkg. (18 oz. total) broccoli slaw (can stretch to two 12 oz. bags if making a bigger batch)
3 green onions, sliced
¼ cup toasted slivered almonds
½ cup dry-roasted sunflower seeds
1 cup dried cranberries or cranraisins
¼ cup water
¼ cup white- or red-wine vinegar
3 Tbsp. extra virgin olive oil
⅓ cup sugar
Ramen seasoning

Break up Ramen noodles. Save seasoning from ramen noodles for dressing. In large bowl, combine all ingredients through cranberries. In a separate small bowl combine dressing ingredients. Gently stir all ingredients together.

Carole Guthrie

LEMON-ARTICHOKE CHICKEN SALAD

This is different, but very good. I served this recipe on a small croissant or stuff a tomato with it.

½ cup mayonnaise
3 Tbsp. peach yogurt
Juice of 2 lemons
¼ cup Parmigiano-Reggiano cheese
1½ cup canned artichoke, drained
3 Tbsp. green onions, chopped (optional)
4 chicken breasts, cooked and cut into bite-sized pieces

Blend mayonnaise, yogurt, lemon juice and cheese in food processor or blender. Add artichokes and pulse until roughly chopped. Stir dressing into chopped chicken a small amount at a time.

Mary Ann Thompson

MAKE AHEAD MARINATED BROCCOLI-CAULIFLOWER SALAD

1 bunch broccoli, cut into bite-sized pieces
1 head cauliflower, cut into bite-sized pieces
1 onion, chopped (to taste)
1 cup mayonnaise
1 Tbsp. sugar
1 tsp. salt
1 tsp. vinegar

Place veggies in a sealable bowl. Mix mayonnaise, sugar, salt and vinegar and pour over veggies. Marinate overnight.

Jayne Martin

MIXED GREENS WITH FETA AND DRIED CRANBERRIES

6-8 cups mixed greens or green leaf lettuce, torn into bite-sized pieces
½ cup cranberries, diced
1 cup toasted walnuts, chopped
1 cup feta cheese
½ cup olive oil
¼ cup cider vinegar
¼ cup sugar
½ medium onion, chopped very fine
½ tsp. paprika
¼ tsp. dry mustard
⅛ tsp. pepper
¼ tsp. celery salt

Combine greens, cranberries, walnuts and cheese. Whisk remaining ingredients to mix, then toss to coat salad.

Ashley Blackburn

RED RASPBERRY SALAD

1 - 10 oz. pkg. frozen raspberries, thawed
2 - 3 oz. pkg. raspberry Jell-O
2 cups boiling water
1 pint vanilla ice cream
1 – 6 oz. frozen pink lemonade, thawed
¼ cup pecans, chopped

Drain raspberries, reserving syrup. Dissolve Jell-O in water and add ice cream. After it melts, stir in lemonade and syrup from raspberries. Chill until slightly set. Add raspberries and pecans and pour into 6-cup ring. Chill overnight or until set.

Cory McCormick

MJ'S ORIENTAL CHICKEN AND SPINACH SALAD

DRESSING
¼ cup vegetable oil
3 Tbsp. rice vinegar
¾ Tbsp. Splenda or 1½ Tbsp. sugar
1 Tbsp. light soy sauce
1 tsp. dark sesame oil
¾ tsp. grated gingerroot
1 pkg. dry mix from Ramen noodles

Whisk all ingredients until combined. Refrigerate, covered, 1 hour to allow flavors to blend.

SALAD
1- 6 oz. baby spinach leaves
2 cups chicken breast, cooked and cubed
2 pkg. Ramen noodles cooked without the dry mix
(the second package of dry mix could be added to the dressing, if you like)
1- 11 oz. can mandarin oranges, drained
½ cup sliced water chestnuts
¼ cup thinly sliced green onions
¼ cup toasted slivered almonds
¼ - ½ bag chow mein noodles

Gently toss all ingredients in large salad bowl. Add dressing and toss to combine.

Marni Johnson

KAY'S DOZIER'S POTATO SALAD

SALAD
6 - 8 cooking potatoes, cook, cool and dice
2 hard-boiled eggs, sliced
½ cup celery, diced
½ cup onion, diced
½ cup yellow bell pepper, diced
Celery Salt
Dill
Pepper
Fresh basil

DRESSING
1 Tbsp. white vinegar
1 Tbsp. horseradish
1 Tbsp. or more raw natural sugar
½ cup reduced mayonnaise or less
¼ cup olive oil

Mix dressing well, then pour over potatoes, spices and veggies. Use paprika over top of salad and garnish with hard-boiled egg slices. Chill for several hours.

Kay Dozier

RED POTATO SALAD

2 lbs. red potatoes
1 cup chopped fresh parsley
1 cup green onion
⅓ cup black olives, sliced
½ cup olive oil
½ cup red wine vinegar
Salt and pepper

Boil potatoes and cut into pieces. Mix all ingredients together, refrigerate before serving.

Nancy Tuberty

QUINOA SALAD WITH DRIED FRUIT AND NUTS

1 cup quinoa
¼ tsp. salt
2 ½ cups chicken stock (or substitute water)
3 green onions, chopped
½ cup craisins and/or dried apricots
1 pinch cayenne pepper
1 Tbsp. vegetable oil
1 Tbsp. rice wine vinegar, or substitute apple cider vinegar
2 Tbsp. lemon juice
2 Tbsp. sesame oil (optional)
⅓ cup fresh cilantro, chopped
¾ cup toasted pecans or walnuts, chopped

Bring the quinoa, salt and water to a boil in a saucepan. Reduce heat to medium-low, cover, and simmer until the quinoa is tender, 20 to 25 minutes. Once done, transfer into a large serving bowl, and let cool for 20 minutes. Once cool, stir in the green onions, craisins, apricots, cayenne pepper, vegetable oil, vinegar, lemon juice and sesame oil. Let sit at room temperature for 1 hour to allow the flavors to blend. Just before serving, stir in the cilantro and pecans.

Holly Moore

SISTER-IN-LAW SALAD

DRESSING
⅓ cup red wine vinegar
2/3 cup oil
½ cup sugar (can cut this in half for a not-so-sweet taste)
1 tsp. dry mustard
1 tsp. poppy seed
½ tsp. garlic salt
Mix together and refrigerate overnight. Shake well before using.
Toss with greens just before serving.

SALAD
2 bags romaine/iceberg lettuce mix
1 cup red grapes, halved
1 cup shredded Swiss cheese (or Mozzarella/Provolone mix can be used)
1 cup cashew pieces
¼ lb. bacon, cooked and crumbled

Nancy Tuberty
The Bereavement Committee of St. Philip

SPINACH AND STRAWBERRY SALAD WITH WISCONSIN GOUDA CHEESE

¼ cup orange juice
3 Tbsp. vegetable oil
1 Tbsp. honey
1 tsp. orange peel, grated
¼ teaspoon garlic salt
⅛ tsp. paprika
4 cups spinach leaves
1 pint strawberries, stemmed and halved
1 cup Wisconsin Gouda cheese, cubed
½ cup pecan or walnut halves or almond slices

In a small, tight-lidded container, combine the orange juice, oil, honey, orange peel, garlic salt and paprika for dressing; cover tightly. Shake well; set aside.

In a large salad bowl, toss spinach leaves, strawberries, Gouda cheese and nuts with dressing. Refrigerate for later, or serve immediately.

Mary Grindstaff

SPINACH SALAD WITH BACON DRESSING

5 slices bacon
1½ Tbsp. shallot, finely chopped
½ cup red wine vinegar
2 Tbsp. honey mustard, or more to taste
Salt and freshly ground black pepper
8 cups fresh spinach leaves, stems removed
8 oz. white button mushrooms (about 2 ½ cups), thinly sliced
½ red onion, thinly sliced

In a skillet add the bacon and cook over medium heat until crisp. Using a slotted spoon transfer the bacon to a paper towel lined plate to drain. Roughly chop and set aside. Pour off all but 2 tablespoons of fat from the skillet. Heat the remaining fat over medium-high heat, add the shallots and cook for 2 minutes, stirring occasionally. Whisk in the vinegar, desired amount of mustard, and salt and pepper, to taste. Scrape the brown bits from the bottom of the skillet, bring to a simmer, then remove the skillet from the heat. For the salad, in a large salad bowl, toss together the spinach, mushrooms, bacon and onion. Pour the dressing over the salad and toss to combine. Serve warm.

Kay Dozier

SEASONED SLAW

2 pkgs. Ramen noodles, chicken flavor
1 pkg. slivered almonds
1 small jar sesame seeds
1 to 2 Tbsp. butter
Dressing:
½ cup oil
½ cup soy sauce
½ cup sugar
¼ cup vinegar
2 pre-packaged bags coleslaw
Green onions, chopped

Crush the noodles and toast with almonds and sesame seeds in butter. Mix with coleslaw and green onions. Boil together the two seasoning packages from the noodles with the oil, soy sauce, sugar and vinegar for 2 to 3 minutes. Toss with the warmed dressing and serve immediately.

Sharon Wilson

SUMMER PASTA SALAD

1-16 oz. package penne pasta
1 cup distilled white vinegar
½ cup white sugar
1-16 oz. bottle Catalina salad dressing
1 cup Italian-style salad dressing
1 cucumber, chopped
2-2 oz. cans sliced black olives
1 tomato, chopped
½ cup onion, chopped
1 cup baby carrots, chopped
1 green bell pepper, chopped
½ tsp. celery salt
Salt and pepper to taste

Bring a large pot of lightly salted water to a boil. Add pasta and cook for 8 to 10 minutes or until al dente; drain.
In a small saucepan, bring vinegar and sugar to a boil. Boil for one minute.
In large bowl, combine vinegar mixture, Catalina dressing and Italian dressing. Mix well. Add pasta, cucumber, olives, tomato, onion, carrots, and bell pepper; toss. Season with celery salt, salt and pepper. Refrigerate until serving.

Sharon Wilson

TOMATO MOZZARELLA SALAD

As tasty as it is pretty! In fact so pretty, it's pictured on the back cover.

Fresh Mozzarella cheese, sliced
Vine-ripened summer tomatoes, sliced (don't bother with winter ones)
Fresh basil
Extra-virgin olive oil
Balsamic vinegar
Salt and pepper to taste

Alternate slices of cheese, basil and tomato. Drizzle lightly with olive oil and balsamic vinegar—don't drown out the flavor of the cheese. Salt and pepper to taste.

Margie Thessin

Vegetables and Side Dishes

OVERNIGHT ASPARAGUS STRATA

1 lb. fresh asparagus, trimmed and cut into 1-inch pieces
4 English muffins, split and toasted
2 cups shredded Colby-Monterey Jack cheese divided
1 cup fully cooked country or regular ham, diced
½ cup sweet red bell pepper, chopped
8 eggs
2 cups milk
1 tsp. salt
1 tsp. ground mustard
¼ tsp. pepper

In a large saucepan, bring 8 cups water to a boil. Add asparagus, cover and cook for 6 minutes. Drain and immediately place asparagus in ice water. Drain and pat dry.
Arrange six English muffin halves, cut side up, in a greased 13 x 9 x 2-inch baking dish. Fill in spaces with remaining muffin halves. Sprinkle with 1 cup cheese, asparagus, ham and red pepper. In a bowl, whisk the eggs, milk, salt, mustard and pepper; pour over muffins. Cover and refrigerate overnight.
Remove from the refrigerator 30 minutes before baking. Sprinkle with remaining cheese. Bake uncovered at 375° for 40 to 45 minutes or until a knife inserted near the edge comes out clean. Let stand for 5 minutes before cutting.

Kay Dozier

BETTIE'S GREEN BEAN CASSEROLE

⅓ cup onion, minced
2 Tbsp. butter
2 Tbsp. flour
½ tsp. salt
½ tsp. pepper
1 cup sour cream
2 cups French style green beans, drained
½ cup Cheddar cheese, grated

Simmer onion and melted butter, then add flour, salt and pepper. Add sour cream and heat. Add beans and top with cheese. Bake at 350° for 30 minutes.

Carole Guthrie

BROWN RICE

1 cup white rice
1 stick butter, melted
1 can Campbell's beef consommé
1 can Campbell's French onion soup
Green onions, chopped (to taste)
½ cup toasted pine nuts

Melt butter in 2-quart casserole dish while preheating the oven to 350°. Mix and add the other ingredients and cook for approximately 45 minutes. Add green onions and pine nuts.

Sally Nance

CANDIED CARROTS

4 Tbsp. unsalted butter
¼ cup maple syrup
⅛ tsp. kosher salt
⅛ tsp. cayenne pepper
¼ cup water
1½ pound carrots, halved lengthwise
⅛ tsp. black pepper

Melt butter in a large saucepan over medium heat. Add the maple syrup, salt, cayenne and water, and bring to a boil. Add the carrots and return to a boil. Reduce heat, and simmer, turning occasionally, until the carrots are tender and the liquid is reduced to a glaze, 15 to 20 minutes. Season with black pepper.

Stacie Mullen

CAROLE'S COLORADO BEANS

8 slices of real bacon
2 large onions, chopped
½ cup brown sugar
½ cup vinegar
2- 15 oz. cans lima beans
1 can pork & beans
1 can kidney beans
1 can great northern beans (or any canned beans you like!)

Fry bacon. Remove bacon and cook onions in bacon drippings until transparent. Add sugar and vinegar. Drain all beans except pork & beans. In large bowl combine bacon, onion, beans and crumbled bacon. Bake in 2 quart casserole at 325° for 1 hour.

Carole Guthrie

CHEESE (OR GARLIC) GRITS

From Taffy Hairston a sweet friend who said the grits can be cooled, halved and frozen for another meal

2 cup grits (regular)
1½ qt. water
2- 6 oz. rolls of garlic cheese or 2 rolls of sharp Cheddar cheese, cut up into small pieces
½ cup milk
4 eggs, beaten
½ cup butter or margarine
Salt and pepper to taste
Parmesan cheese, grated
Paprika

Preheat oven to 300°. Bring water to boil, add grits and let thicken. Add cheese, milk, eggs, butter, salt and pepper. Mix well. Pour into buttered 4-quart casserole dish. Sprinkle with Parmesan cheese and paprika. Bake for 30 to 45 minutes.

Missy Rudman

CORN CASSEROLE

½ cup margarine
2 eggs, slightly beaten
8 oz. sour cream
1-17 oz. can whole kernel corn, drained
1-17 oz. can creamed corn
1- 8 oz. pkg. corn muffin mix

Set oven to 350 degrees. While it heats, put margarine into a 1½-quart casserole (I usually use a glass 9 x 13-inch) and place in oven to melt. Remove from oven as soon as margarine is melted. In a bowl, beat eggs and then mix with sour cream. Stir in all corn and muffin mix. Bake at 350° for about 40 minutes or until set.

Karen Updike

CORN PUDDING

1 can creamed corn
1 can whole kernel yellow corn, drained
5 Tbsp. flour
1 Tbsp. sugar
¼ cup butter or margarine, melted
¾ cup milk
3 eggs

Whisk corn, flour and sugar. Add and mix butter or margarine, milk and eggs. Bake for 1 hour at 325° in buttered dish.
To double recipe, use 13 x 9-inch casserole and bake at 325° for 1 hour and 30 minutes.

Marge Ellis

CORN SOUFFLE

1 box Jiffy cornbread mix
1 can cream corn
1 can whole kernel corn, drained
½ cup salad oil
¼ cup sugar
8 oz. sour cream
Salt and pepper to taste

Mix together and bake in a 9 x 13-inch greased pan at 350° for one hour.

Nancy Tuberty

DITO D'ORO (OVEN-FRIED EGGPLANT)

This is a good Lenten dish.

¾ cup seasoned breadcrumbs
¼ cup Parmesan cheese, freshly grated
1 medium eggplant, peeled and sliced into 1 x 4-inch squares
½ cup oil

Preheat oven to 375°. Line baking sheet with foil. Combine bread crumbs and Parmesan cheese. Toss eggplant strips in oil and roll in breadcrumb mixture. Place on baking sheet and bake about 15 to 20 minutes. Sprinkle with additional Parmesan cheese and serve immediately.

Judy Tujague

GRILLED ONION

Sweet Vidalia Onion (or other sweet onion)
1 tsp. butter
1 beef bouillon cube

Cut top and bottom from onion and pull skin off. Scoop a small teaspoonful from onion top. Put pat of butter into the hole and push bouillon cube into that. Wrap onion with aluminum foil tightly. Place on heated grill for 30 minutes. If onion is very large may need 35 minutes.

Bob Rudman

EGGPLANT PARMESAN

Adapted from Southern Living 1984 Annual Recipes.

1 cup onion, chopped
1 clove garlic, minced
2 Tbsp. olive oil
1-16 oz. can whole tomatoes, undrained and chopped
1- 8 oz. can tomato sauce
1 tsp. salt, divided
½ tsp. dried basil
½ tsp. dried oregano
1 large eggplant
1 2/3 cup Progresso Italian breadcrumbs
2 eggs, beaten
½ cup vegetable oil
1- 8 oz. pkg. sliced mozzarella cheese
½ cup grated Parmesan cheese

Sauté onion and garlic in olive oil in a skillet until tender. Stir in tomatoes, tomato sauce, ½ teaspoon salt, basil and oregano. Cover and bring to a boil. Reduce heat and simmer 20 minutes, stirring the mixture occasionally.

Peel eggplant, if desired. Cut eggplant crosswise into ½-inch slices. Combine breadcrumbs and ½ teaspoon salt. Dip eggplant slices in eggs; coat with breadcrumbs. Sauté in hot oil (375°) until golden brown, turning once. Drain.

Spoon half of tomato sauce mixture into a 13 x 9 x 2 inch baking dish. Arrange eggplant over sauce; top with cheese slices and remaining sauce. Sprinkle with Parmesan cheese. Bake at 400° for 10 minutes.

Nancy M. Jantz

STREBEL FAMILY GERMAN POTATO SALAD

5 lbs. red potatoes
2 medium onions, chopped
1½ lb. bacon, thick sliced
1¼ cup white vinegar
1½ cup sugar
2½ cups water
1 tsp. white pepper
2 Tbsp. Coleman's yellow mustard powder
2 Tbsp. dried parsley leaves
5 heaping Tbsp. flour

Put potatoes in large kettle of water and boil until you can stick a fork in largest potato and can easily pull it out. Remove potatoes from heat, drain and run cold water over the potatoes until they can be handled. Remove peel from potatoes, then cut into bite-sized pieces and place in 5 quart casserole.

Put bacon on a cutting board and dice it first the long way, then top to bottom. Put in deep skillet and set heat on medium-high. When bacon is cooked but not browning, remove skillet from heat and spoon off all but 4 to 5 tablespoons of bacon fat and discard. Return skillet to heat and add onions. Turn heat down to medium. Make sure bacon and onion do not brown. When onion bits are translucent turn down to low.

Add vinegar, sugar, half of the water, flour, white pepper, mustard powder and parsley leaves to a shaker. Cover tightly and shake until well mixed. Pour mixture into pan with bacon and onions and add remaining water. Shake and add to pan and stir well. Turn heat to medium-high until mixture starts bubbling then reduce heat to medium and allow to cook for about 10 to 12 minutes. Sauce will thicken. Continue stirring. Turn off heat, pour sauce mix over potatoes and gently mix in until potatoes are covered. Keep warm in 200° oven until ready to be served.

Jerry Strebel

FRESH CRANBERRY MOLD

I obtained this recipe from St. Eugene Parish cookbook in Santa Rosa, California about 40 years ago. It has always been enjoyed, so I hope members of Serra Club of Williamson County will enjoy it. It's simple to make and is always a big hit.

2 cups water
¾ cup sugar
1 pkg. fresh cranberries
1- 6 oz. package Jell-o, either raspberry or cranraspberry
1- 8 oz. can crushed pineapple
½ cup celery, chopped
½ cup walnuts or pecans, chopped

Heat water and sugar to boiling in a 2 quart saucepan; add cranberries and cook at boiling for 5 minutes. Stir in Jell-o until dissolved. Remove from heat and stir in pineapple, celery and walnuts. Pour into a mold and refrigerate until firm.

Josephine Taormina

MARINATED ASPARAGUS

Great for vegetable side dish at luncheon or hors d'oeuvre.

Fresh asparagus
Chives
Pesto salad dressing (or Cardini Light Greek Vinaigrette)

Tie 2 to 3 stalks of asparagus together with chive. Lightly steam asparagus bundles. Place single-layer flat in a pan and pour pesto dressing over asparagus. Set overnight in refrigerator covered.

Cory McCormick

MAC AND CHEESE

1 Tbsp. vegetable oil
1- 16 oz. pkg. elbow macaroni
9 Tbsp. butter
1 cup Muenster cheese, shredded
1 cup mild Cheddar cheese, shredded
1 cup sharp Cheddar cheese, shredded
1 cup Monterey Jack cheese, shredded
1½ cups half & half
2 eggs, beaten
¼ tsp. salt
⅛ tsp. ground black pepper

Bring a large pot of lightly salted water to a boil. Add the oil and the pasta and cook for 8 to 10 minutes or until al dente; drain well and return to cooking pot. In a small saucepan over medium heat, melt 8 tablespoons butter; stir into the macaroni. In a large bowl, combine the cheeses; mix well. Preheat oven to 350°. Add the half & half, 4 cups of cheese mixture, and eggs to macaroni; mix together and season with salt and pepper. Transfer to a lightly greased deep 2½ to 3-quart casserole dish. Sprinkle some more cheese if desired on top and 1 tablespoon of butter.
Bake for 35 minutes or until hot and bubbling around the edges; serve.

Ruth Ann Graveno

ORZO WITH PARMESAN AND BASIL

2 Tbsp. butter
1 cup uncooked orzo pasta
1-14.5 oz. can chicken broth
½ cup grated Parmesan cheese
¼ cup chopped fresh basil
Salt and pepper to taste
2 Tbsp. chopped fresh basil

Melt butter in heavy skillet over medium-high heat. Stir in orzo and sauté until lightly browned. Stir in chicken stock and bring to boil. Cover. Reduce heat and simmer until orzo is tender and liquid is absorbed, about 15 - 20 minutes. Mix in Parmesan cheese and basil. Season with salt and pepper. Transfer to shallow bowl. Garnish with basil sprigs.

Sharon Wilson

MACARONI AND CHEESE

¼ cup butter or margarine, divided
2 cups elbow macaroni, cooked
¼ cup flour
½ cup Cheddar cheese, shredded
1 cup milk
6 Ritz crackers crushed (about ¼ cup)
½ lb. Velveeta cheese, cubed

Heat oven to 350°. Melt 3 tablespoons butter in medium saucepan on medium heat. Whisk in flour, cook 2 minutes stirring constantly. Gradually stir in milk. Bring to boil: cook and stir 3 to 5 minutes or until thickened. Add Velveeta, cook 3 minutes or until melted, stirring frequently. Stir in macaroni. Spoon into greased or sprayed 2 quart casserole; sprinkle with Cheddar cheese. Melt remaining butter, toss with cracker crumbs. Sprinkle over casserole. Bake 20 minutes or until heated thoroughly.

Paddy Gerbic

MEXICAN RICE

2 cups long grain rice
2 Tbsp. oil
¼ cup onion, chopped
1 garlic clove, chopped (or ½ Tbsp. garlic powder)
½ cup tomato, chopped

½ cup celery, chopped
4 oz. unsalted tomato sauce
4 cups chicken broth
¼ tsp. ground pepper
¼ tsp. ground cumin
¼ tsp. salt

In medium saucepan, heat oil on medium heat then add rice and sauté until clear. Add onion and garlic, sauté for 2 minutes, add tomato and celery and sauté for 1 minute, add rest of the ingredients, bring to boil, cook for 20 minutes in low heat or until liquid is gone.

Ana Anaya

MICROWAVE SPINACH CASSEROLE

Microwave spinach is a pot luck favorite of mine. Since I originally took it to our Homeowners' Association Pot Luck, I have had to bring it every time—by popular request.

2 pkg. frozen chopped spinach
1 can Durkee or French's French fried onions
1 small can cream of mushroom soup
1 small can chopped or sliced mushrooms
8-9 oz. jar Cheez Whiz Jalapenos or Velveeta Mexican

Boil spinach according to package directions omitting salt. Melt in microwave mushroom soup and cheese, about 5 minutes. Drain spinach. Combine all ingredients and mix well. When ready to serve, microwave on high for 5 minutes.

Mary Anderson

ONION BREAD PUDDING

Good as a side dish.

1 Vidalia onion sliced
2 cups 2% milk
½ tsp. salt
½ tsp. thyme
⅛ tsp. black pepper
2 large eggs
8 cups French bread, cubed
¾ cup shredded Gruyere or Swiss cheese, divided
Cooking spray

Preheat oven to 425°. Heat large non-stick skillet over medium-high heat. Add onion slices and brown. Combine milk, eggs and seasonings. Add bread and ½ cup cheese. Mix well. Place ½ of mixture in 8" square dish that has been coated with cooking spray. Arrange onion slices over this, add rest of mixture and top with onions and cheese. Cook for 25 minutes.

Missy Rudman

MISSION INN POTATOES

This goes great with ham. I don't know where I got the recipe, but many years ago I entered it in a Franklin Review-Appeal *recipe contest and won 1st prize, $15.00!!!*

6 medium potatoes, peeled and sliced ¼ inch thick
1 medium onion, sliced
1 clove garlic, diced
1 tsp. salt
1 tsp. beef bouillon
1 lb. Cheddar cheese, shredded
1- 4 oz. can green chilies, seeded and diced
1 cup sour cream
1 egg
Paprika

Boil water in saucepan, adding potatoes, onion, garlic, salt and beef bouillon. Return to boil, stirring. Lower heat and cook covered 10 to 12 minutes until almost tender.

Pour half of the potatoes and liquid into a shallow 2-quart casserole or 13 x 9-inch pan.

Cover with half of the shredded cheddar cheese and half of the chilies. Top with remaining potato mixture and the remaining cheese, reserving 2 tablespoons of the cheese.

Bake at 350° for 20 minutes. Remove from oven. Mix sour cream (at room temperature) and 1 egg, lightly beaten. Spread over the top of the potatoes. Arrange remaining chilies and the remaining cheese on the sour cream layer. Sprinkle with paprika. Bake 10 minutes until golden brown. Let stand 15 minutes before serving.

Marge Swauger

ORANGE-PECAN GREEN BEANS

This is delicious. You may need to double or triple.

8 oz. fresh green beans, trimmed, cut in half crosswise
2 Tbsp. fresh orange juice
1 Tbsp. Dijon mustard
1 tsp. light brown sugar
2 Tbsp. unsalted butter
1 small red onion, very thinly sliced
⅓ cup pecans, coarsely chopped
½-¾ tsp. salt
Freshly ground pepper
½ tsp. fresh thyme, lightly chopped

Bring water to a boil, add salt and beans. Cook 4 to 5 minutes; drain and rinse under very cold water. Drain well on paper towels.

In a small bowl, whisk together orange juice, mustard and brown sugar. In large skillet, melt butter and sauté onions and pecans, until onions are shrunken and many are browned, about 8 to10 minutes. Add beans in one layer over contents of the pan and season with salt, pepper and thyme. Add the mustard mixture, turn to medium low and stir and toss together. Sauce should thicken slightly. Heat beans thoroughly, 1 to 2 minutes.

.

Mary Ann Thompson

POTATO CASSEROLE

1- 2 lb. bag diced hash browns, thawed
1 cup onion, diced
1 can cream of chicken soup
1- 1 lb. carton sour cream
1 stick butter, melted
8 oz. sharp Cheddar cheese, grated
Crushed potato chips

Mix everything together except for chips and put in a greased 9 x 13-inch pan. Top with potato chips. Bake for one hour at 370°.

Marcia Petsch

ROASTED HARVESTED VEGETABLES

¼ cup extra virgin olive oil
¼ cup vegetable broth
1 tsp. salt
¼ tsp. pepper
½ lbs. carrots, peeled
½ lbs. Brussels sprouts, ends cut diagonally into ½ inch pieces and trimmed and halved
½ lb. fingerling potatoes, halved
1 medium butternut squash, cut in half lengthwise, quartered if large, peeled and diced

Preheat oven to 400°. Line jelly roll pan with foil. In large bowl, mix olive oil, broth, salt and pepper then toss with mixed vegetables to coat. Drain and save remaining broth mixture, then spread the vegetables on the pan. Pour the reserved broth mixture over the vegetables. Roast for 35 to 40 minutes or until tender, stirring once.

Paddy Gerbic

RATATOUILLE

1 lg. onion, chopped
1 green pepper, sliced
¾ lb. eggplant, diced
2 zucchini or crook neck squash, sliced and diced
1 lb. ripe tomatoes, chopped
¼ tsp. garlic powder
2 tsp. dried basil
1 tsp salt
¼ tsp. pepper

Combine all ingredients in a large pot such as a Dutch oven. Bring to a boil and then simmer to desired texture. The above ingredients can be increased or decreased to suit your taste. Serve with or without rice.

Jayne Martin

SQUASH CASSEROLE

My late husband loved making this recipe and hearing the compliments that came with it.

2 cups squash, cooked and drained
1 onion, cut into small pieces (cooked with the squash)
1 can mushroom soup
Salt and pepper to taste
1 stick of butter melted
2 cups mild Cheddar cheese, grated
3 eggs, beaten
½ cup crushed Ritz crackers

Mix all ingredients except crackers. Place in a baking dish that has been sprayed with Pam. Sprinkle with cracker crumbs on casserole and bake at 350° for 35 to 40 minutes.

Sally Nance

SPINACH, RICE AND FETA PIE

This is good for Lent.

2 tsp. margarine
¾ cup onion, chopped
2 tsp. flour
½ tsp. salt
¼ tsp. pepper
2 Tbsp. Parmesan cheese
Cooking spray

2 cup cooked long-grain rice
¾ cup feta cheese, crumbled
1 lg. egg, lightly beaten
2 lg. egg whites
1- 10 oz. pkg. frozen chopped spinach, thawed, drained, squeezed dry

Preheat oven to 400°. Melt margarine over medium heat and add onion. Sauté 3 minutes. Stir in flour, salt and pepper. Gradually add milk stirring with wire whisk until well blended. Bring to simmer and cook 1 minute until slightly thick, stirring constantly. Remove from heat, stir in rice, feta, eggs and spinach. Pour into 9-inch pie dish coated with cooking spray. Sprinkle Parmesan cheese on top. Bake 35 minutes or until set. Broil 2 minutes or until golden brown.

Judy Tujague

CREAM CHEESE BASIL SUMMER SQUASH

3 yellow squash, cubed
1 clove garlic, minced
1-(8 oz. package cream cheese, cubed)
1 Tbsp. dried basil leaves
Salt to taste

In a glass serving dish, combine the squash pieces and garlic. Season with salt, cover with plastic wrap, and microwave for 5 to 8 minutes on high, or until tender. Stir after every 3 to 4 minutes.
Sprinkle the cream cheese over the top, and return to the microwave, uncovered for about 1 minute, or until the cheese is melted. Stir until the cheese is smooth and blended into the squash. Let set for a minute or two before serving.

Sharon Wilson

SWEET AND SOUR GREEN BEANS

2 lb. green beans, trimmed or 3 cans cut drained green beans
8 slices bacon
1 small red onion, chopped
½ cup apple cider vinegar
½ cup sugar or Splenda
Salt and pepper to taste

Place the green beans into boiling water and cook, covered, for 20 minutes or until tender. Drain.

Cook the bacon until crisp. Remove bacon from pan, drain on paper towels. Add onion into bacon fat. Cook until translucent. Add vinegar, sugar and salt to onions. Stir to mix well making sure sugar is completely dissolved. Add the beans to onion mixture. Cook to warm through. Plate and crumble bacon on top to serve.

Teresa A. Jones

SWEET POTATO CASSEROLE

3 sweet potatoes, baked
1 stick margarine or butter
1 cup granulated sugar
½ cup evaporated milk
3 eggs, well beaten
3 tsp. vanilla extract
Lots of cinnamon to taste
1 cup brown sugar
½ cup self rising flour
½ cup chopped nuts
1 stick oleo or butter, melted

Blend potatoes, margarine or butter, sugar, milk, eggs, vanilla extract and cinnamon together until smooth. Pour into a greased 11x13-inch casserole. Mix remaining ingredients and pour on top. Bake 1 hour at 300°.

Jean Berry

SWEET ONION CASSEROLE

4 lg. onions, sliced
1 cup Ritz cracker crumbs
1 ½ cups cheddar cheese, grated
1 can cream of mushroom soup

Layer first 3 ingredients. Pour soup on top (sometimes I add milk). Bake at 350° for 1 hour.

Phyllis Hesse

YUM YUM YAMS

3 cups canned sweet potatoes, roughly 2 – 29 oz. cans
1 stick butter
¾ cup sugar
2 eggs, beaten
1 tsp. vanilla extract
1 cup brown sugar
⅓ cup flour
1 cup pecans, chopped
⅓ cup butter, softened, not melted

Preheat oven to 350°. In medium bowl, mix potatoes, butter, sugar, eggs and vanilla extract and pour into buttered casserole dish.
In small bowl, mix brown sugar, flour and nuts and sprinkle over the yams. Cut butter into small bits and distribute over topping. Bake for 20 minutes.

Sarah Crockett Watkins

ZUCHINNI, SQUASH AND TOMATOES

4 squash sliced
2 zucchini, sliced
2 large cans whole tomatoes
1 medium onion, slivered
Garlic powder to taste
Parsley to taste
Pepper to taste
1 cup rice (optional)

Combine ingredients and bring to a quick boil. Reduce heat to a simmer. Cook for at least 1 hour.

Ruth Ann Graveno

ZUCCHINI BORDELAISE

This recipe requires tiny zucchini, which are difficult to find. For best results with a regular-sized zucchini, cut zucchini into rounds ¼-inch thick.

1½ lb. small zucchini
2 Tbsp. olive oil
½ tsp. salt
Freshly ground pepper (6 turns of the pepper mill)
2 Tbsp. fresh bread crumbs
1 Tbsp. butter
2 Tbsp. shallots, chopped
4 Tbsp. fresh parsley, chopped

Rinse the zucchini and pat them dry. Trim off the ends, but do not peel them. Heat the oil in a nonstick frying pan and, when it is hot, add the zucchini. Sauté the zucchini over the high heat, shaking the pan and tossing the vegetables gently. Add the salt and pepper. Cook a total of 5 minutes.
Add the bread crumbs and butter to the pan. When the crumbs start to brown, add the shallots and toss the mixture for another minute. Serve the zucchini hot, sprinkled with the parsley.

Claire Garland

Pasta

CHICKEN TORTELLINI

½ stick butter
1-8 oz. pkg. tortellini
8 oz. Monterey Jack cheese, shredded
4 chicken breasts, cut into bite-sized pieces
Flour
¾ cup onion, chopped
1 Tbsp. chicken bouillon granules or 2 cubes
1-8 oz. can chicken broth
1 Tbsp. sugar
1- 4 oz. can mushrooms
½ cup sour cream

Cook tortellini according to directions. Spray 8 ½ x 11 inch pan with cooking spray. Pour tortellini in pan. Add ½ the cheese over pasta. Roll the chicken in flour and brown in butter. Place browned chicken on top of pasta. Cook onion in butter. Add bouillon, broth, sugar and mushrooms with liquid to onions. Bring to a slow boil and cook for 5 minutes. Add remaining cheese to boiling liquid. Remove from heat and add sour cream. Pour liquid over chicken with pasta. Cover and bake at 350° for 45 minutes.

Christine Grisham

BOW TIE PASTA

1-16 oz. pkg. bowtie pasta
2 green onions, chopped
1 6 oz. pkg. feta cheese, crumbled
½ cup balsamic vinegar
¼ cup olive oil
2 cups chopped fresh tomato

Cook pasta for 8-10 minutes until al dente. Drain and place in ice water to cool. Toss pasta with onions, cheese, balsamic vinegar, olive oil, cheese, balsamic vinegar, olive oil and tomatoes.

Sharon Wilson

LUPINI

1 16-oz box rotini noodles
1 30-oz. jar spaghetti sauce
1 carton ricotta cheese
1 egg
1 Tbsp. parsley
¼ cup Parmesan cheese

Mix ricotta cheese, egg, salt, pepper, parsley and parmesan cheese.

Cook rotini noodles according to package directions.
Spread a thin layer of spaghetti sauce in bottom of 9x13" pan. Set aside.

Mixed cooked noodles and cheese mixture; spread over sauce. Cover with remaining sauce. Sprinkle with parmesan cheese. Cover and bake at 350° for 30 minutes.

Sharon Wilson

Here are three great lasagna recipes, including one from the head of the Diocese of Nashville and reputed gourmet cook, Bishop David R. Choby.

THE BEST LASAGNA EVER

One of Bishop Choby's favorite recipes (and Elizabeth, his secretary, loves it, too!)

1 lb. sweet Italian sausage
¾ pound lean ground beef
½ cup minced onion
2 cloves garlic, crushed
1-28 oz. can crushed tomatoes
2 -6 oz. cans tomato paste
2 -6.5 oz. cans canned tomato sauce
½ cup water
2 Tbsp. white sugar
1½ tsp. dried basil leaves
½ tsp. fennel seeds
1 tsp. Italian seasoning
1½ tsp. salt, divided
¼ tsp ground black pepper
4 Tbsp. chopped fresh parsley
12 lasagna noodles
16 oz. ricotta cheese
1 egg
½ tsp. salt
¾ lb. mozzarella cheese, sliced
¾ cup grated Parmesan cheese

In a Dutch oven, cook sausage, ground beef, onion, and garlic over medium heat until well browned. Stir in crushed tomatoes, tomato paste, tomato sauce, and water. Season with sugar, basil, fennel seeds, Italian seasoning, 1 teaspoon salt, pepper, and 2 tablespoons parsley. Simmer, covered, for about 1½ hours, stirring occasionally.

Bring a large pot of lightly salted water to a boil. Cook lasagna noodles in boiling water for 8 to 10 minutes. Drain noodles, and rinse with cold water. In a mixing bowl, combine ricotta cheese with egg, remaining parsley, and ½ salt.

Preheat oven to 375°

To assemble, spread 1½ cups of meat sauce in the bottom of a 9 x 13-inch baking dish. Arrange 6 noodles lengthwise over meat sauce. Spread with one half of the ricotta cheese mixture. Top with a third of mozzarella cheese slices. Spoon 1½ cups meat sauce over mozzarella, and sprinkle with ¼ cup Parmesan cheese. Repeat layers, and top with remaining mozzarella and Parmesan cheese. Cover with foil: to prevent sticking, either spray foil with cooking spray, or make sure the foil does not touch the cheese.

Bake in preheated oven for 25 minutes. Remove foil, and bake an additional 25 minutes.

Cool for 15 minutes before serving

Bishop David Choby

LASAGNA

SAUCE
1 lb. ground chuck
½ lb. bulk Italian sausage
1 medium onion, chopped
1 heaping teaspoon minced garlic
1 -32 oz. jar Ragu spaghetti sauce with mushrooms
1 -15½ oz. jar Ragu pizza sauce
1 Tbsp. parsley flakes
1 tsp. oregano
2 tsp. Italian seasoning spices
¼ cup Parmesan cheese, grated

Brown the ground chuck and sausage; add onion and garlic and cook until onion is transparent. Drain. Add the rest of the sauce ingredients and simmer about ½ hour.

NOODLES
Cook 9 lasagna noodles as directed on the package. Be sure to rinse well in cold water and drain thoroughly.

CHEESE
1 -15½ oz. pkg. Ricotta cheese
¼ cup Parmesan cheese, grated
1 Tbsp. parsley flakes
1½ tsp. salt
1½ tsp. oregano
Mix together in a small bowl.

MOZARELLA
2 cups Mozzarella cheese

Reserving about ¾ cup of sauce for the top, spray a 9 x 13-inch casserole with Pam. Barely coat the bottom of the dish with sauce. Lay 3 noodles in pan to cover the bottom. Layer ⅓ of remaining sauce, Ricotta cheese mixture and Mozzarella cheese onto noodles. Repeat 2 more times. Spoon reserved sauce on top and sprinkle with ¼ cup Parmesan cheese. Bake uncovered in a 350° oven for 45 minutes. Let stand at least 15 minutes before serving. You can cool and freeze it for 3 weeks or less. To serve, cook uncovered in a 375° degree oven until bubbly, about 1 hour.

Karen Updike

SPINACH LASAGNA

I love this because you don't cook noodles beforehand!

16 oz. small curd cottage cheese
2 cups Mozzarella/Monterey Jack cheese, shredded (reserve some for topping)
1 egg
1- 10 oz. pkg. chopped spinach, thawed and drained
½ tsp. salt
¾ tsp. oregano
⅛ tsp. pepper
½ cup water
32 oz. spaghetti sauce
9 lasagna noodles, uncooked

Preheat oven to 350°. Mix cottage cheese, egg, cheese, spinach and seasoning in a bowl. Pour ¾ cup tomato sauce onto bottom of a 9 x 13-inch baking dish and spread. Then layer with noodles, cheese mixture and tomato sauce. Top with noodles, sauce and some shredded cheese. Pour water in corners of the dish. Cover dish with foil (tenting if possible) and bake for 1 hour. Let stand for 15 minutes and then serve. Even better if made the day before.

Missy Rudman

PANCIT CANTON (STIR-FRIED NOODLES)

A Filipino noodle dish of Chinese origin. It's served during special occasions such as birthdays (for long life because of the long noodles).

1 lb. flour sticks or pancit canton (found in Asian stores)
2 Tbsp. oyster sauce
1 Tbsp. garlic, minced
1 tsp. ground black pepper
4 cups chicken stock or broth
1 tbsp. salt
4 Tbsp. soy sauce
2 cups cabbage, thinly sliced or julienned
2 cups carrots, julienned
1 lb. chicken breast, sliced (may use pork) (may boil chicken then shred meat)
8 pieces medium-sized shrimp (optional)
1 cup onion, sliced
1 cup celery, julienned
1½ cups snow peas, sliced
2 Tbsp. cooking oil
Lemon

In wok or pan, heat the oil and sauté garlic and onion. Add the chicken or pork and cook till light brown. Add the soy sauce and cook for 5 minutes. Put in shrimp, oyster sauce and chicken stock and simmer for 20 minutes. While simmering, blanch all vegetables in a separate pot. Add salt and pepper to taste. Put in flour sticks and cook till all liquid has been absorbed by the noodles. Add all the blanched vegetables and mix with the rest of the ingredients.
Serve hot and squeeze lemon over it before eating.

Poy Dacpano

PIZZA AND MARINARA SAUCE

DOUGH
½ cup warm water (105°)
2 tsp. of dry yeast
2 cups flour
1 tsp. salt
3 Tbsp. olive oil

Mix water and yeast; let stand 5 minutes. Mix flour and salt; blend in oil. Add yeast mixture then knead on floured surface until smooth, about 1 minute.

Transfer dough to oiled bowl. Cover with plastic wrap and set aside for 1 hour until it doubles. Punch down dough. Makes one 16-ounce ball. Cook pizza at 450°. (sprinkle pan with cornmeal for 15 minutes.

MARINARA SAUCE FOR PIZZA AND PASTA
½ cup olive oil (or less)
2 small onions, finely chopped
2 garlic cloves, finely chopped
2 celery stalks, finely chopped
2 carrots, peeled and finely chopped
½ tsp. sea salt
½ tsp. pepper
½ tsp. fennel (optional)
2 – 32 oz. cans crushed or fresh tomatoes
2 dried bay leaves

Sauté all veggies in olive oil for 10 minutes. Add tomatoes and bay leaves and simmer uncovered on low heat for about 1 hour (until the sauce thickens). Freeze or use right away!

Kay Dozier

ORECCHIETTE WITH MINI CHICKEN MEATBALLS
We love this recipe from Giada de Laurentis

1 lb. orecchiette pasta
¼ cup plain bread crumbs
¼ cup fresh flat parsley, chopped
2 lg. eggs, lightly beaten
1 Tbsp. whole milk
1 Tbsp. ketchup
¾ cup freshly grated Romano cheese
½ tsp salt
¾ tsp. pepper
1 lb. ground chicken
¼ cup olive oil
1½ cups low sodium chicken broth
4 cups cherry tomatoes, halved
1 cup fresh grated Parmesan cheese
8 oz. bocconicini (small mozzarella balls), halved
1 cup chopped fresh basil leaves

Bring a large pot of salted water to a boil over high heat. Add the pasta and cook until tender, about 8 to 10 minutes.

In a medium bowl, stir together bread crumbs, parsley, eggs, milk, ketchup, Romano cheese, salt and pepper. Add chicken and combine well. Using a melon baller to scoop the mixture, roll the seasoned chicken into ¾-inch mini meatballs.

Heat oil in a large skillet over medium-high heat. Working in batches, add meatballs and cook without moving until browned on the bottom, about 2 minutes. Turn meatballs and brown the tops for 2 more minutes. Add chicken broth and tomatoes and bring to a boil, using a wooden spoon to scrape the brown bits that cling to the bottom of the pan.

Reduce the heat to low and simmer until the tomatoes are soft and the meatballs are cooked through, about 5 minutes. Drain the pasta, reserve 1 cup of the pasta water. Transfer the pasta to a large serving bowl and add ½ cup of Parmesan cheese. Toss to coat the pasta lightly, adding some of the reserved pasta water to help make a sauce. Add the meatball mixture, bocconcini, and ½ cup of the basil. Combine. Garnish with the remaining basil and cheese.

Patti Caprara

SPAGHETTI RING

1½ cups cooked spaghetti
Salt and pepper to taste
1 cup Cheddar cheese, shredded
1 cup white bread, crumbled
1- 12 oz. jar pimento
1 egg, beaten
3 Tbsp. parsley, minced
1 cup milk
1 onion, minced
3 Tbsp. butter
Peas, mushrooms or water chestnuts (optional)

Break spaghetti into quarters and cook. Drain spaghetti. Preheat oven to 350°. Mix spaghetti and cheese. Add pimento, parsley, onion, salt and pepper. Mix well. Add bread and egg. Heat milk until hot then add butter and mix. Pour into spaghetti mixture and mix well. Spray a 10-inch ring pan with Pam and pour spaghetti into ring. Set ring in a pan of water and bake for 40 minutes. Invert spaghetti ring onto a platter and fill center with green peas, mushrooms or water chestnuts.

Alice Spaulding
Alma de la Guardia

Main Courses

Poultry

BAKED CHICKEN AND RICE WITH BLACK BEANS

1-10 oz. pkg. yellow rice mix
1 cup onion, chopped
½ cup green bell pepper, chopped
½ cup carrot, chopped
1 Tbsp. olive oil
2 cups chicken, cooked and cubed
1-15 oz. can black beans, drained
1-10 oz. can diced tomatoes and green chilies, undrained
2 cups Monterey Jack cheese, grated

Preheat oven to 350°. Prepare rice according to package directions. Meanwhile, sauté onion, bell pepper, and carrot in hot oil in a medium skillet over medium heat 10 minutes or until tender. Combine hot cooked rice, onion mixture, chicken, beans, diced tomatoes and chilies, and 1½ cups cheese in a large bowl. Spoon into a lightly greased 3 quart or 13 x 9-inch baking dish; sprinkle with remaining cheese. Bake, covered, at 350° for 30 minutes; uncover and bake 10 minutes or until cheese is melted.

Mary Grindstaff

BAKED CRUNCHY ONION CHICKEN

2 cups French's fried onion rings
2 Tbsp. flour
6 to 8 boneless skinless chicken strips
3 to 4 Tbsp. prepared mustard, any kind

Crush onion rings with flour in a large Ziploc bag. Dip chicken in mustard and coat in bag to cover all sides of chicken. Place in baking dish (sprayed lightly with Pam olive oil) Bake in 400° oven for 20 minutes or until no longer pink in center.

Jane Harrington

BALSAMIC CHICKEN

4 boneless skinless chicken breasts
1 lb. mushrooms, quartered
2 Tbsp. flour
Salt and pepper to taste
2 Tbsp. olive oil
6 cloves garlic, peeled
¼ to ⅓ cup balsamic vinegar
¾ cup chicken broth
1 bay leaf
¼ tsp. dried thyme
1 Tbsp. butter

Season flour with salt and pepper. Dredge breasts in flour. Shake off excess. Heat oil in skillet over medium-high heat. Cook chicken about 3 minutes per side or until browned. Add the garlic and mushrooms. Cook about 3 more minutes. Add vinegar, broth, bay leaf and thyme. Cover and cook over medium-high heat for 10 minutes. Turn the chicken occasionally. Transfer chicken to platter. Keep warm. Cook the sauce, uncovered, on high heat for about 7 minutes. Stir frequently, swirl in butter. Remove the bay leaf and garlic. Add chicken to reheat. Goes well with pasta or rice.

Edme Mendez

CARAMELIZED CHICKEN WITH CRANBERRY CONSERVE

3 Tbsp. frozen orange juice concentrate, thawed
2 Tbsp. balsamic vinegar
2 Tbsp. dry sherry
1 garlic clove, minced
4 boneless skinless chicken breast halves
3 Tbsp. brown sugar
1 Tbsp. dark sesame oil
1 small onion, chopped
½ cup dried cranberries
1–2 Tbsp. sesame seeds, toasted (optional)
1–2 Tbsp. green onions, minced (optional)

Combine first 4 ingredients in a heavy duty Ziploc bag. Add chicken. Seal and chill for at least an hour. Remove chicken from marinade, reserving marinade. Cook brown sugar and sesame oil in a large nonstick skillet over medium-high heat, stirring constantly, 4 minutes.

Add chicken and cook 3 to 4 minutes on each side. Add reserved marinade, onion and cranberries; cook, stirring and turning chicken often, 10 minutes or until chicken is done. Remove chicken and let stand for 5 minutes. Slice and serve with cranberry mixture. Sprinkle with sesame seeds and green onions, if desired.

Christine Grisham

CHICKEN OR PORK ADOBO OR MIX

This is an authentic Filipino dish. Not to be mistaken for the Mexican Adobo, this dish is uniquely prepared by stewing chicken or pork in vinegar and soy sauce.

2 lbs. chicken or pork, cut into serving pieces
3 bay leaves
4 Tbsp. soy sauce
2 Tbsp. vinegar
3 cloves garlic, crushed
1-2 cups water
¼ cup cooking oil
½ Tbsp. white sugar
Salt and whole peppercorn

In a large container, combine the soy sauce and garlic then marinade the chicken or pork for at least 3 hours. Heat oil in pan. When the oil is hot enough, put in the marinated chicken or pork. Cook all the sides for about 5 minutes. Pour in the remaining marinade and add water. Bring to a boil. Add the bay leaves and whole peppercorns. Simmer for 30 minutes or until meat is tender. Add vinegar. Stir and cook for 10 minutes. Put in the sugar and salt. Stir and turn off heat. Serve hot with rice.

Poy Dacpano

CHICKEN BROCCOLI CARROT CASSEROLE

1 cup broccoli, chopped
1 cup carrots, sliced
1 cup chicken, chopped
1 can cream of chicken soup
½ cup sour cream
1 cup Pepperidge Farm seasoned croutons
1 Tbsp. flour
1 Tbsp. minced onion
2 Tbsp. margarine, melted

Cook vegetables and chicken. Combine the soup, sour cream, croutons, flour, onion and margarine. Add the drained vegetables and chicken to the above combined ingredients.
Place in 9 x 9-inch baking dish and bake at 350° for 30 minutes until bubbly.

Sheri Isham

CHICKEN ALMOND CASSEROLE

1 cup chicken, cooked and chopped
1 cup celery, chopped
½ cup slivered almonds, lightly toasted
½ cup mayonnaise
1- 4 oz. can sliced mushrooms, drained
1- 2 oz. jar pimento
2 hard-boiled eggs, chopped
1 Tbsp. onion, chopped
1- 10 ¾ oz. can cream of chicken soup
½ cup cracker crumbs

In a bowl combine all ingredients except cracker crumbs. Pour into a 2-quart casserole. Sprinkle cracker crumbs on top. Bake at 350° for 30 minutes.

Ashley Blackburn

QUICK CHICKEN CACCIATORE

1 pkg. skinless boneless chicken thighs
2 Tbsp. olive oil
½ cup onion, chopped
1- 14½ oz. can Italian-style stewed tomatoes, undrained
½ cup dry white wine or chicken broth
Salt and pepper to taste

Trim visible fat from chicken. In a large nonstick skillet, over medium heat, heat oil. Add chicken and brown 2 minutes on one side, turn and add onion to skillet. Cook 2 minutes longer or until chicken is browned and onions are golden, stirring occasionally. Stir in tomatoes, wine, salt and pepper. Reduce heat to medium-low. Cover and simmer 10 to 15 minutes or until chicken is tender and sauce has thickened slightly. Serve over spaghetti if desired.

Paddy Gerbic

CHICKEN AND NOODLES

1 pkg. wide noodles
3 chicken breasts
2 chicken bouillon cubes
2 cups water
Celery tops
1 carrot, shredded
1- 10½ oz. can cream of mushroom soup
Salt, pepper and tarragon to taste

Cook egg noodles according to package directions. Boil chicken breasts in water with bouillon cubes, celery tops and carrot for flavoring. Mix cooked chicken and noodles with cream of mushroom soup. Season with salt, pepper and tarragon.

Cory McCormick

CHICKEN LICKIN' CASSEROLE
Easy and tasty

2 cans condensed creamed soup (any combination of chicken, celery, mushroom and asparagus)
1 can water
1 cup regular rice
3 to 4 lb. pkg. cut up boneless chicken

Preheat oven to 350°. Spray a 13 x 9-inch baking pan with cooking spray. Mix the soups, water and the rice in a bowl and pour into the prepared baking pan. Place chicken parts on top of the soup/rice mixture. Bake for 1 hour. HINT: Add about a cup of frozen mixed vegetables or other vegetable for variations.

Claudia Finnegan

CILANTRO LIME CHICKEN

1- 24 oz. jar medium or mild salsa
Juice of 1 lime
¼ cup fresh cilantro, chopped
1- 1.25 oz. pkg. taco seasoning
2 jalapeno peppers, finely chopped (optional)
4-6 boneless chicken breast halves

In a slow cooker, mix together salsa, lime, cilantro, taco seasoning and peppers. Add the chicken to the slow cooker and coat with the salsa mixture. Cover and cook on low for 6 hours. Serve the chicken with the salsa mixture spooned over the top. You can also add sour cream and tortilla chips.

Lindsey Garansuay

CRANBERRY CHICKEN

1 can whole cranberry sauce
1- 8 oz. bottle of French dressing
1 packet of Lipton onion soup mix
1 lb. chicken, cut into bite-sized pieces

Put all together in a baking dish and bake 350° for 60 to 90 minutes and serve over rice.
During the summer, when I don't want to use the oven, I cook the chicken in a frying pan then add all the ingredients and simmer for 20 minutes.

Jayne Martin

CURRY CHICKEN

I always double this recipe....as my family loves it.

½ cup of butter
1 large onion, peeled and sliced
2 garlic cloves, peeled and sliced
1 tsp. coriander powder
1 tsp. turmeric powder
1 tsp. chili powder
½ tsp. salt
1 tsp. ground black pepper
1½ cup raw chicken, cut in bite- sized pieces (lamb, fish or vegetables can be substituted for chicken)
1 cup water
1 tsp. Garam Masala (can be found in international section of market)

Melt butter in a pan, add the onion and garlic and sauté gently until soft but not brown. Stir in the coriander, turmeric, chili, salt and pepper. Add raw chicken pieces, fry for 5 minutes then add the water and bring to a boil. Lower the heat and simmer for 20 minutes, then add the Garam Masala and simmer for another 5 minutes. Serve hot, spooned over a bowl of rice.

Sally Nance

ENCHILADAS VERDES DE POLLO

2 Tbsp. cooking oil
12 corn tortillas
2 cups cooked chicken, shredded
2 cups Monterey Jack cheese, shredded
¾ cup onion, chopped
¼ cup butter or margarine
¼ cup all-purpose flour
2 cups chicken broth
1- 4 oz. can pickled jalapeno peppers, rinsed, seeded and chopped
½ tsp. salt
1 cup sour cream
1 medium tomato, finely chopped
½ cup onion, finely chopped

In small skillet heat oil. Dip each tortilla in hot oil for 10 seconds or just till limp. Drain on paper towel. Place 2 tablespoons of the shredded chicken, 2 tablespoons cheese and 1 tablespoon onion on each tortilla, roll up. Place rolls seam side down in 13 x 9 x 2-inch baking dish.

In medium saucepan melt butter or margarine; blend in flour. Add chicken broth all at once; cook, stirring constantly, till thickened and bubbly. Reserve 1 tablespoon chopped peppers. Stir sour cream and remaining peppers into sauce; cook till heated through but do not boil. Pour sauce over rolled tortillas in baking dish.

Bake in 425° for 20 minutes. Sprinkle remaining shredded cheese atop tortillas, return to oven for about 5 minutes or till cheese melts. Top with tomato and onion when served.

Ana Anaya

FAVORITE BRING-TO-NEW-MAMA CHICKEN POT PIE

This delicious comfort food was first brought to me after my fourth child was born. I love to bring it to others when I can. My own family rarely gets it, but we all love it when that rare occurrence happens.

4-6 chicken breasts, cooked and cut into bite sized pieces	2 cups carrots, sliced
	2 cups onion, chopped
1⅓ cup butter	4 cups chicken broth
1 cup flour	2 cups milk
1- 2 pack Pillsbury pie crust	2 tsp. salt
2 cups celery, chopped	½ tsp. black pepper

Stir together chicken broth, milk, salt and black pepper. Sauté vegetables in butter until tender, approximately 10 minutes. Add flour. Cook over medium heat, stirring constantly, for 1 minute. Slowly add broth-milk mixture. Cook over medium heat, stirring constantly, until thickened and bubbly. Add cooked chicken. Stir. Pour into 2 casserole dishes. Top with Pillsbury pie crust pastry, rolled to fit pan. Bake at 400° for 30 minutes.

Erin Morel

JANIE'S "HUG" CASSEROLE

4 chicken breasts, cooked and cut into pieces	1 cup sour cream
	1 cup cheddar cheese
1 pkg. frozen broccoli spears or cuts (cooked)	Grated onion to taste
	Curry to taste (optional)
1- 10½ oz. can cream of chicken soup	
½ cup mayonnaise	

Mix all but chicken, then add chicken. Bake at 350° for 45 minutes.

Carole Guthrie

NEW ENGLAND POT PIE

8 chicken breasts
1 large can sliced carrots
1 pkg. frozen peas
1 jar pearl onions (I use Aunt Nellie's)
3 tsp. parsley, snipped
3 Tbsp. butter
1 cup half & half
3 Tbsp. flour
¼ tsp. pepper
1 can chicken broth
1 pie crust

Cook chicken breasts and cut into chunks. In bowl combine chicken, carrots, peas, onions and parsley (don't defrost peas). Melt butter, stir in flour and pepper and cook 2 to 3 minutes, stirring constantly. Remove from heat and stir in half & half and chicken broth. Cook until thickened. Pour over chicken mixture and cover with pie crust. Bake at 425° for 10 minutes, then 350° for 45 minutes.

Barbara Valentine

PARMESAN CHICKEN
This is easy to prepare and is elegant.

Chicken breasts
Butter
Garlic powder
Bread crumbs
Parmesan cheese

Dip chicken breasts in melted butter with a dash of garlic powder, and then roll in a mixture of equal parts dried bread crumbs and Parmesan cheese. Place in a shallow baking dish and bake at 375° for 45 minutes or until browned.

Nancy Tuberty

OVEN BAKED CHICKEN FAJITAS

1 lb. boneless skinless chicken breasts, cut into strips
2 Tbsp. vegetable oil
2 tsp. chili powder
2 tsp. cumin
½ tsp. garlic powder
½ tsp. dried oregano
¼ tsp. salt
1-15 oz. can diced tomatoes with green chilies
1 medium onion, sliced
1 large bell pepper, seeded and sliced (I use half a green and half a red)
12 flour tortillas
Toppings such as cheese, sour cream, and guacamole, if desired

Preheat oven to 400°. Place chicken strips in a greased 13 × 9 inch baking dish. In a small bowl combine the oil, chili powder, cumin, garlic powder, dried oregano and salt. Drizzle the spice mixture over the chicken and stir to coat. Next add the tomatoes, peppers and onions to the dish and stir to combine. Bake uncovered for 20 to 25 minutes or until chicken is cooked through and the vegetables are tender. Serve on tortillas with desired toppings.

Mary Grindstaff

SWEET SOUR CHICKEN

6 - 9 chicken breasts
1- 10 oz. jar apricot preserves
Salt and pepper to taste
1-8 oz. bottle Russian dressing
1 pkg. onion soup mix
1 cube beef bouillon, dissolved in ¼ cup hot water

Place chicken in a 9 x 13-inch pan. Mix all remaining ingredients together and pour over chicken. Cook at 350° for 1 hour.

Rosemary Strawn

PARMESEAN CRUSTED BRUSCHETTA CHICKEN

⅓ cup mayonnaise with olive oil
3 Tbsp. Parmesan cheese, grated
4 boneless skinless chicken breast halves
4 tsp. plain dry bread crumbs
1 Tbsp. Italian seasoning
2 medium tomatoes, seeded and chopped
¼ cup red onion, chopped
¼ cup Italian dressing

Preheat oven to 425°. Combine mayonnaise with cheese in medium bowl. Arrange chicken on baking sheet and evenly coat with mayonnaise mixture. Sprinkle with bread crumbs and Italian seasoning. Bake 20 minutes or until chicken is thoroughly cooked. Meanwhile, combine remaining ingredients in a bowl and top chicken with bruschetta mixture to serve.

Terry Bies

POLLO AL POMODORO

2- 8 oz. chicken breasts
Flour, seasoned with salt and pepper
¼ cup butter
2 garlic cloves, chopped
⅛ tsp. thyme
⅛ tsp. basil
1 tomato, chopped
2 green onions, chopped
1 cup white wine or chicken broth
½ lb. linguine, cooked
Parmesan cheese

Pound chicken breasts. Dredge chicken in flour, then sear in butter. Set chicken aside. Add garlic, thyme, basil, tomato, onions and wine or chicken broth to pan. Simmer for 5 minutes. Add chicken back to pan and serve over linguine with Parmesan cheese.

Louise Volpe

POPPY SEED CHICKEN

4 - 5 chicken breasts
2- 10.5 oz. cans of cream of chicken soup (or 1 each cream of chicken and 1 cream of celery)
8 oz. sour cream
¾ cup margarine, melted
2 Tbsp. poppy seeds
1 sleeve Ritz crackers

Cook chicken in salt water, then cut into bite size pieces and layer in 13 x 9-inch casserole dish. Mix soup and sour cream, and pour over the chicken in the casserole dish. Crush Ritz crackers. Mix margarine, poppy seeds and the crushed crackers. Top the casserole with the cracker topping. Bake at 305° for 30 minutes.

Marge Ellis

TURKEY AND WILD RICE STEW

Leftover Thanksgiving turkey (or any leftover turkey)
1 cup wild rice
6 Tbsp. margarine
2 Tbsp. flour
2 lb. mushrooms
½ cup onion, chopped
2 cup celery, chopped
3 cups chicken broth
1½ cups heavy cream
Salt and pepper to taste

Cook wild rice according the package directions. Authentic wild rice will need an hour to cook using 1 cup wild rice to 3 cups water. Melt 3 tablespoons margarine in skillet. Add mushrooms, onion, celery and sauté over medium heat. Set aside.
In a large pan, melt 3 tablespoons margarine and add flour to make a paste. Slowly add chicken broth then add heavy cream. Salt and pepper to taste. Add wild rice, turkey, mushrooms, onion and celery. Heat and serve.

Sheri Isham

SLOW COOKER CHICKEN WITH OLIVES

I love slow cooker recipes and this one is delicious. I get compliments every time I make it!

12 chicken thighs, about 4 pounds, skinned
1 tsp. kosher salt, divided
¼ tsp. freshly ground black pepper, divided
1 tsp. olive oil
1½ Tbsp. minced garlic
¼ cup dry white wine
3 Tbsp. tomato paste
2 -3 tsp. crushed red pepper
1- 28 oz. can diced tomatoes, drained
¼ cup sliced pitted Kalamata olives
2 Tbsp. fresh flat-leaf parsley, chopped

Sprinkle chicken with ½ teaspoon salt and ⅛ teaspoon black pepper. Heat oil in a large skillet over medium-high heat. Add chicken to pan; cook 2 minutes on each side or until browned. Place chicken in an electric slow cooker. Add garlic to pan, and sauté 30 seconds, stirring constantly. Add wine, scraping pan to loosen browned bits; cook 30 seconds. Place wine mixture in cooker. Add tomato paste, crushed red pepper, and tomatoes to cooker. Cover and cook on high 4 hours. Stir in remaining ½ teaspoon salt, remaining ⅛ teaspoon pepper, olives, and parsley. Serve over brown rice.

Stephanie Carroll

SPICY CHICKEN AND VEGETABLE STIR-FRY WITH THAI BASIL

1 cup brown rice
2 cups water (for the rice)
2 boneless chicken breasts
1 large yellow or white onion
3 large whole carrots
10 large white mushrooms
1 large head broccoli
2 Tbsp. peanut oil
1 tsp. sesame oil
2 Tbsp. low-sodium soy sauce
1 tsp. Asian fish sauce
1½ tsp. hot sauce (You can choose which sauce and adjust the quantity to taste. I use a very hot habanero sauce or Sriracha.)
1 tsp. rice vinegar
¼ cup water (for the sauce)
¼ cup water (for the corn starch)
1 Tbsp. corn starch (for thickening)
2 cloves garlic
½ cup fresh Thai basil leaves

Bring the water set aside for the rice to a boil in a medium or large pot and add the rice. Typically you cover the rice and let it simmer on low for 45 minutes or so, so do this first. If you prefer, you can use a rice cooker for this step. Note: For a low-carbohydrate diet, you can skip the rice altogether.

When the rice is about 20 minutes from being done, start the rest of the meal. Cut the chicken into ½ inch cubes and set aside. Wash the carrots, broccoli, mushrooms, and Thai basil. If the basil has stems, remove, keeping only the leaves. Peel and dice the onion, peel and slice the carrots into ½ inch sections, and slice the very bottom off the stem of each mushroom.

Remove the large stems from the broccoli head, and cut into tiny trees about 1½ inch tall. Set each prepared ingredient aside in its own container. Add peanut and sesame oil to a large wok or non-stick skillet. Heat on medium-high. When the oil is hot add the chicken. Allow to cook until the chicken just barely begins to brown, stirring often. Add the onions, stir, wait a few seconds, add the carrots. Cook and stir for 1 minute, then add the broccoli. Cook for 1 more minute, stirring often. Add the mushrooms.

Mix the sauce by stirring the soy sauce, fish sauce, rice vinegar, hot sauce, and water together in a small bowl. Slowly add the sauce to the rest of the ingredients. Cook for eight minutes, constantly stirring.

Mix corn starch and water together in a small bowl and stir until all the corn starch melts into the water. Add the corn starch mixture and cook until sauce thickens somewhat. Turn off heat. Press the cloves of garlic and add them. Coarsely shred and add the Thai basil leaves. Stir. Allow to cool and thicken for five minutes.

To plate, spoon rice onto a plate and flatten. Spoon the stir fry on top of the rice.

James Hamilton

TANDOORI CHICKEN

2 lbs. chicken drumsticks
½ cup yogurt
3 Tbsp. tandoori paste or tandoori powder
1 Tbsp. lemon juice
1 Tbsp. lime juice
1 Tbsp. turmeric powder
1 Tbsp. coriander powder
1 Tbsp. cinnamon powder
4 Tbsp. butter
1 Tbsp. red pepper powder
Salt and pepper to taste
¼ cup onion, sliced fine
1 Tbsp. ginger paste
1 Tbsp. garlic paste

First boil the chicken drumsticks. Discard the broth. Using a fork, poke holes into the chicken after it is boiled. Mix all ingredients except chicken and butter in a blender. Mix well. It will become like a paste. If it is not red or orange color, add more tandoori paste. Marinate the chicken in the mixture overnight or for at least two hours in the refrigerator. Be sure to rub the mix into the chicken before marinating.

Place chicken in a pan. Take two tablespoons of the butter and divide it around the chicken. Cook chicken in 450 degree oven for 20 minutes. After 15 minutes, turn the chicken and add the remaining butter, to keep the chicken moist.

Eat warm with drinks or other food.

Fr. Bala

UNSTUFFED PEPPER CASSEROLE
This makes a lot and freezes well.

2 cups cooked brown rice
1 box frozen spinach
1 onion
1 each green, red and yellow pepper
2 tsp. minced garlic (4 cloves)
20 baby carrots
1 Tbsp. olive oil
1 lb. ground turkey breast
2 tsp. Mrs. Dash or similar
2 tsp. oregano
1- 29 oz. can stewed or crushed tomatoes
14 oz. low sodium chicken broth
½ cup grated Parmesan cheese (optional)

Thaw spinach. Chunk veggies. Heat oil and sauté veggies in garlic. Crumble the meat, break up the spinach and add both to the sauté. While waiting for meat to brown, add seasonings to sauté. Once browned, add tomatoes and broth. Once mixture comes to a boil add rice and cheese. Stir well. Simmer 15 minutes.

Patti Caprara

Pork

GOURMET PORK CHOPS

6 loin pork chops, ½ inch thick
2 Tbsp. flour
1 tsp. salt
Dash pepper
2 Tbsp. shortening
1- 10 ½ oz. can cream of mushroom soup
¾ cup water
½ tsp. ground ginger
¼ tsp. dried rosemary, crushed
1-3½ oz. can French-fried onions
½ cup sour cream

Coat chops with flour, salt and pepper mixture. Brown on both sides in hot shortening. Place in casserole.

Combine soup, water, ginger and rosemary. Pour over chops. Sprinkle with half the onions. Cover and bake at 350° degrees for 50 minutes or until meat is tender. Uncover and sprinkle with remaining onions and continue baking 10 minutes.

Remove meat to platter. Blend sour cream into soup mixture in casserole. Heat. Serve with meat.

Donna DeCoster

BARBARA'S ROAST PORK TENDERLOIN

2-3 pork tenderloins, approximately 1½ lbs each
1 Tbsp. butter
½ cup real maple syrup
½ cup ketchup
¾ cup water
¼ tsp. salt
¼ tsp. celery salt
1½ Tbsp. flour
½ cup water

Dust tenderloin with flour, salt and pepper. Brown slowly in butter. Mix syrup, ketchup, ¼ cup water, salt and celery salt for sauce. Pour over browned meat in covered pan. Cover and bake for 1½ hours at 350°. Remove pork to platter. Add flour mixed with remaining water, shaking to thicken, to sauce remaining in pan. Stir to mix. Slice pork; pour sauce over tenderloin before serving.

Carole Guthrie

GORTON

This is a French meat used in sandwiches.

2 lbs. fatty ground pork
½ tsp. salt
¼ tsp. cloves

1 whole onion, peeled
Pepper to taste
½ tsp. cinnamon

Place all ingredients in a sauce pan and cover with cold water. Bring to a boil, stirring often; let it simmer until all water has evaporated and meat starts to stick to pan. Remember to stir often. Remove onion and pour remainder into containers about the size of a sandwich container. Let cool in containers before covering them and putting them in the fridge. After several hours the meat will look like cooked ground pork with lots of fat. When ready to make sandwiches, use like lunch meat or grill like grilled cheese sandwiches.

Yvette Woods

JACK DANIEL'S PORK TENDERLOIN

MARINADE
¼ cup soy sauce
¼ cup bourbon
2 Tbsp. brown sugar

Marinate 1 pkg. pork tenderloins for at least 2 hours.

Bake meat only in pan at 325° for 45 minutes and then grill for crispness. Serve with mustard sauce.

MUSTARD SAUCE
2/3 cup sour cream
2/3 cup mayonnaise
2 Tbsp. dry mustard
3-4 green onion, finely chopped

Sharon Wilson

JERK RIBS

2 lbs. pork ribs
2 Tbsp. dried minced onion
1 Tbsp. onion powder
4 tsp. ground thyme
2 tsp. salt
2 tsp. ground allspice
½ tsp. ground nutmeg
½ tsp. ground cinnamon
1 Tbsp. sugar
2 tsp. black pepper
1 tsp. cayenne

In small jar with tight-fitting lid, shake together all dry ingredients until well-blended. Rub dry mixture onto all surfaces of ribs.
Grill ribs over indirect heat in covered grill, turning occasionally, until ribs are very tender, about 1½ hours (or roast ribs on rack in shallow pan in 350° oven for 1½ hours).
Cut into 1 or 2-rib portions to serve.

Sharon Wilson

PORK NORMANDIE

2 ½ lbs. pork sirloin, cut into 2 inch cubes
1 tsp. herbes de Provence
¼ cup Dijon mustard
Salt and pepper to taste
½ cup all-purpose flour
⅓ cup olive oil
1 large onion, chopped
1 large Granny Smith apple, peeled, cored, quartered and sliced
3-4 garlic cloves, minced
2 cups fresh apple cider
¼ cup Calvados (apple brandy)
Freshly cooked egg noodles

Combine pork cubes, herbes de Provence and mustard with salt and pepper in a large bowl. Cover, refrigerate several hours or overnight. Shake pork pieces a few at a time in flour. Heat oil in large skillet and sauté pork in batches, do not crowd. Transfer to platter and pour off all but 3 tablespoons of drippings from pan.

Sauté onion, apple and garlic till soft, about 5 minutes. Return pork to pan. Pour in cider and Calvados. Bring to a boil, lower heat, cover. Simmer for 1 hour or until pork is tender. Serve with egg noodles.

Terry Bies

PORK ROAST

4-5 lb. pork loin, boned and rolled
2 Tbsp. wet mustard
2 tsp. thyme
½ cup sherry
½ cup soy sauce
¼ tsp. garlic powder
1 tsp. ginger

Rub meat with mustard and thyme. Combine sherry, soy sauce, garlic powder and ginger and pour over meat. Refrigerate overnight. Cook uncovered at 325° for 2½ to 3 hours.

For a sauce, combine the following:
2- 10 oz. jars of black currant jelly
2 Tbsp. soy sauce
3 Tbsp. sherry

Barbara Valentine

TUSCAN PORK ROAST

5 to 8 garlic cloves, peeled
1 Tbsp. dried rosemary
1 Tbsp. olive oil
½ tsp. salt
1 3-4 pound boneless pork loin roast

In a blender or food processor, combine garlic, rosemary, oil and salt; blend until mixture turns to paste. Rub over the roast; cover and let stand for 30 minutes.

Place on a greased baking rack, fat side up, in a roasting pan. Bake, uncovered, at 325° for 2 to 2½ hours or until a meat thermometer reads 160°-170°. Let stand for 15 minutes before slicing.

Sharon Wilson

STUFFED PORK LOIN

2 lb. boneless pork loin
1 medium onion, chopped
¼ cup white vinegar
2 Tbsp. olive oil
2 large garlic cloves, chopped
2 tsp. fresh thyme leaves
1 tsp. brown sugar
½ tsp. crushed red pepper
½ tsp. allspice
12 large prunes
½ cup dark rum
Salt and pepper to taste
4 Tbsp. orange marmalade
2 green onions
1 cup chicken stock

Butterfly the pork loin. Blend the onion, vinegar, oil, garlic, thyme, brown sugar, red pepper and allspice and place in a Ziploc bag with pork loin to refrigerate overnight, turning occasionally. Combine the prunes with the rum and soak for 3 hours.

Preheat oven to 350°. Place loin in a 13 x 9-inch baking dish and bake for 2 hours. Remove from oven, open the loin and add salt and pepper to taste. Thread prunes through 2 thin green onions and place inside loin. Roll up loin. Brush with 1 tablespoon marmalade and cook till meat reaches 160°. Remove meat. Place remaining marmalade and chicken stock into the pan. Scrape down sides of pan and boil till sauce thickens.

Peggy Crockett

Beef

BISTRO SKILLET STEAK

2 tsp. olive or canola oil
1 onion, cut into thin wedges
2 lb. boneless sirloin steak
¾ tsp. salt
½ tsp. freshly ground pepper
¾ cup reduced sodium chicken broth
12 cherry tomatoes, halved (or more to taste)
⅓ cup jarred sliced hot (or mild if preferred) cherry peppers

Heat oil in a 12- inch nonstick skillet over medium-high heat. Add onion and cook 7 to 8 minutes, until browned and almost tender. Transfer to a plate.

Sprinkle both sides of steak with salt and pepper. Add steak to hot skillet; cook 5 minutes per side for medium-rare (cook 7-8 minutes per side for medium). Remove steak from skillet and keep warm.

Add broth, tomatoes, peppers, and onions to skillet; cook 1 to 2 minutes until sauce thickens slightly. Slice steak into thin strips and top with sauce. Serve immediately.

Sue Stacy

BEEF AND GRAVY

¼ lb. dried beef
4 Tbsp. flour
½ stick margarine
1 qt. milk

Brown the dried beef in the margarine in a skillet. Add the flour and mix well until flour is all yellow and slightly browned. Add the milk, stirring constantly until thickened. Add a little black pepper. Serve on toast or boiled, fried or baked potatoes.

Ruth Ann Graveno

BRIDE'S MEAT LOAF

This meatloaf was always a family favorite. It originally came from the newspaper in Cleveland Ohio and I still have the original clipping.

2 lbs. ground beef
½ cup onion, chopped
2 cups high protein cereal (like Special K) or corn flakes
1- 8 oz. can tomato sauce
2 eggs, slightly beaten
2 tsp. salt
1 tsp. oregano
1Tbsp. mustard
1 Tbsp. Worcestershire sauce
1 Tbsp. parsley, chopped (substitute dried parsley)
¼ tsp. pepper

Combine ingredients; mix lightly but thoroughly. Pack into greased 9 x 5 x 3-inch loaf pan. Refrigerate if prepared ahead. Bake in preheated 350° oven 1 hour. (Increase baking time 10 minutes if refrigerated). Let stand 10 minutes before removing from pan. Serve hot or cold. Makes wonderful cold meat loaf sandwiches! May also be baked in slow cooker for 6 to 8 hours.

Mary Anderson

BEEF BRISKET WITH WHIPPED POTATOES AND ASPARAGUS

3-4 lb. beef brisket
1 pkg. onion soup mix
Idaho russet potatoes
Sour cream
Butter
Asparagus
Shallots
Olive oil
Red pepper flakes
Creamy horseradish sauce

Preheat oven to 325°. Trim some of the fat from the brisket, then place it on Reynolds Wrap in a 9 x 13-inch casserole dish. Pour onion soup mix on top of the brisket, and wrap the brisket with the Reynolds Wrap to seal tightly. Cook for 30 minutes; reduce oven temperature to 300° and cook for 3 hours.
Remove brisket from oven and from the casserole dish, and pour off the juice in the foil into a jar. When the brisket is cool, cut off all remaining fat and discard. Re-wrap the meat and place it in another casserole dish. Cover the dish, and store in refrigerator overnight with jar of onion soup liquid.
Next day, slice the brisket while cold into thin slices; form the slices into the brisket shape and place in a casserole dish. Skim fat from soup liquid; pour some of the liquid over meat. Cover the casserole dish and place in the oven. Reheat the brisket at 325° for 30 minutes. The brisket is now ready to serve.
While the meat is in oven, make whipped potatoes and asparagus spears. I recommend Idaho russet potatoes and I use sour cream and one tablespoon of butter to whip the potatoes; salt and pepper to taste.
For the asparagus, I use a shallot, fine chopped, a little olive oil, and a pinch of red pepper flakes.
Creamy horseradish sauce goes well with the brisket as does Red Zinfandel, chilled. Strawberries and cream for dessert.

Bill Kennedy

BRISKET WITH PORTOBELLO MUSHROOMS AND DRIED CRANBERRIES

1 cup dry red wine
1 cup canned beef or chicken broth
½ cup frozen cranberry juice cocktail, thawed
¼ cup all purpose flour
1 large onion, sliced
4 garlic cloves, chopped
1½ Tbsp. fresh rosemary, chopped
1- 4 lb. trimmed flat-cut beef brisket
12 oz. medium Portobello mushrooms, dark gills scraped away and thinly sliced
1 cup dried cranberries

Preheat oven to 300°. Whisk wine, broth, cranberry juice and flour to blend in medium bowl, then pour into a 15 x 10 x 2-inch roasting pan. Mix in onion, garlic and rosemary. Sprinkle brisket on all sides with salt and pepper. Place brisket fat side up in roasting pan Spoon some of wine mixture over. Cover pan tightly with heavy duty foil. Bake brisket until very tender, basting with pan juices every hour, about 3½ hours. Transfer brisket to plate and cool 1 hour. Thinly slice brisket across grain, Arrange slices in pan with sauce, overlapping slightly.

Preheat oven to 350°. Place mushrooms and cranberries in sauce around brisket. Cover pan with foil. Bake until mushrooms are tender and brisket is heated through, 30 to 40 minutes. Transfer all to platter and serve. Brisket can be prepared up to 2 days ahead. Cover and refrigerate.

Terry Bies

GERRY'S MEATLOAF

16 oz. ground beef
16 oz. ground turkey or chicken
1 medium onion, finely chopped
1 small green pepper, finely chopped
1 small red pepper, finely chopped
½ cup oatmeal
1 clove garlic, minced
½ tsp dried basil
½ tsp. salt
½ tsp. thyme
⅛ tsp. pepper
1 egg
¼ cup Parmesan cheese
2 oz. mozzarella cheese
1 cup kernel corn, thawed

In a large roasting pan, with your hands, first mix meats, then add veggies, and last add oats, seasonings, egg, cheeses and corn. Shape into loaf. Bake at least 50 minutes at 350°. Let stand 10 minutes before serving. I cut baking potatoes in half and place them in the perimeter of the roasting pan and press the meat mixture down so that the potatoes and meat mixture touch and bake as above.

Jayne Martin

GRANDMA'S BAR-B-Q BEEF

1½ lb. stew meat, cut into bite-size pieces
¾ cup onion, chopped
¾ cup celery, chopped
¼ cup green pepper, chopped
1 cup carrot, chopped
½ bottle ketchup
1 Tbsp. sugar
Salt and pepper to taste

Cook beef in skillet until no longer pink. Add onion and green pepper and continue to cook till browned. Add remainder of ingredients and cook until tender. Serve on buns.

Cory McCormick

HAMBURGER CASSEROLE

1 lb. ground beef
1 small onion, chopped
8 oz. elbow macaroni
1 can peas
¼ green pepper, chopped
1 can mushrooms
2 -15 oz. cans tomato sauce
Garlic powder, pepper and dried parsley to taste
Romano cheese, grated

Brown meat, onions and pepper. Then add mushrooms, peas and tomato sauce. Turn off heat but leave in the pan until you cook the macaroni. Then combine ingredients and place in a greased casserole dish and top with the cheese. Bake at 350° for about 45 minutes.

Ruth Ann Graveno

ITALIAN BEEF

3-4 lb. sirloin tip roast
1 packet McCormick au jus seasoning packet, blended in 2 cups water
½ bottle pepperocini peppers and liquid
1 fresh green pepper, chopped
1 onion, chopped
2 Tbsp. (jar) jalapeño peppers, chopped or one whole fresh jalapeño chopped
2 Tbsp. fennel seed

Place all ingredients in crock pot for 6-8 hours on high. Serve with crusty rolls.

Lucy Quillen

ITALIAN POT ROAST

1-8 oz. pkg. sliced mushrooms
1 large sweet onion
3-4 lb. boneless chuck roast
1 tsp. pepper
2 Tbsp. olive oil
1 envelope onion soup mix
1-14 oz. can beef broth
1- 8 oz. can tomato sauce
3 Tbsp. tomato paste
1 tsp. dried Italian seasoning
2 Tbsp. corn starch

Place mushrooms and onion in a lightly greased slow cooker. Place roast on top of mushrooms and onion in slow cooker. Sprinkle pepper and onion soup mix over roast. Pour beef broth and tomato sauce over roast. Cover and cook on low for 8 to 10 hours. Transfer roast to cutting board, remove any large pieces of fat. Keep warm.

Combine cornstarch and 2 tablespoons of water, mix until smooth. Add cornstarch and tomato paste to juice in cooker. Increase to high and cook for 40 minutes or until mixture is thickened. Stir in roast.

Ashley Blackburn

LAYERED BEEF AND CABBAGE CASSEROLE

1 large head green cabbage
¼ cup salad oil
¾ tsp. salt
1 lb ground beef
1 small onion, minced
1- 32 oz. jar spaghetti sauce
1 cup water
⅓ cup regular long-grain rice
1- 8 oz. pkg. mozzarella cheese, coarsely shredded

Cut off and discard tough ribs from cabbage leaves and coarsely shred. In 5-quart Dutch oven over medium heat, in hot salad oil, cook cabbage and salt until very tender, stirring occasionally. Meanwhile, prepare meat sauce. In 12-inch skillet over high heat, cook ground beef and onion until pan juices evaporate and meat is well browned, stirring occasionally. Add spaghetti sauce, water and rice; heat to boiling. Reduce heat to low; cover and simmer 20 minutes until rice is tender, stirring occasionally.

Preheat oven to 350°. In 13 x 9-inch baking dish, spoon ½ cup meat sauce. Top with one-half of cabbage, and one-half of cheese. Repeat layering with remaining cabbage, meat sauce, and cheese. Bake 20 minutes or until heated through.

Nancy Downey

MARINADE FOR FLANK STEAK

¼ cup soy sauce
2 Tbsp. vinegar
2 Tbsp. minced onion
1 clove garlic
1½ tsp ginger
¼ cup sugar (or = sugar substitute)

Marinate flank steak overnight and grill.

Carole Guthrie

NO-PEEK STEW

2 lbs. lean chuck, cut in 2 in. cubes
1- 1⅜ oz. pkg. onion soup mix
1-10½ oz. can cream of mushroom soup
1 cup ginger ale or water
1- 4 oz. can sliced mushrooms

Put ingredients in a 2½-quart casserole dish and cover. Bake at 300° for 3 hours. DON'T PEEK!!! Let stand 30 minutes before serving. Serve with cooked rice or noodles. Can also be cooked in crock pot.

Mary Anderson

RICE AND BEEF PORCUPINES

This is always a favorite with my grandchildren.

1 lb. ground beef
3 Tbsp. onion, chopped
½ cup washed raw rice
1 tsp. salt
¼ tsp. poultry seasoning
2 cans tomato sauce
1 cup water
3 Tbsp. oil

Mix all ingredients in oil. Form into small balls and sauté in oil. Drain excess fat from pan and add the water. Cover and simmer 40 to 50 minutes until rice is tender.

Jackie Ellis

STUFFED PEPPERS

3 green peppers
1½ cup rice
1½ tsp. salt
2 stalks celery, finely diced
2 Tbsp. butter or margarine
1 lb. ground beef
1 egg
1- 10¾ oz. can tomato soup
1 Tbsp. parsley flakes
2 Tbsp. onion, chopped
Dash of pepper
1- 6 oz. can tomato paste

Preheat oven to 375°. Cut green peppers in half. Scrape out seeds and light green membrane. Set aside. Cook rice in 1 cup water with ½ teaspoon salt for 10 minutes until partially cooked. Drain.

Sauté celery and onion in butter about 5 minutes. Put beef in large bowl and add the rest of the salt, rice, celery, egg, half the soup and the next four ingredients. Mix well with hands. Fill each pepper cavity with filling and place in casserole. Mix remaining soup, 1½ soup cans of water and the tomato paste. Pour over stuffed peppers.

Cover with lid or foil and bake for 1 hour. Then lower temperature to 350° and bake ½ hour longer.

Louise Volpe

Lamb

We received just one lamb recipe, and it's a winner.

LAMB STEW IN A LOAF

This has been our traditional Christmas Eve meal for many years. You can buy bread bowls from a restaurant such as Panera Bread but the homemade ones are much better. Have the butcher cube the meat for you. Recipe can be doubled, tripled, etc.

1 lb. lean lamb, cut into 1 inch cubes
2 Tbsp. all-purpose flour
2 Tbsp. olive or vegetable oil
1 large tomato, peeled and coarsely chopped
¾ cup water
1 tsp. beef flavored bouillon granules
1 small bay leaf, crumbled
½ tsp. chili powder
⅛ tsp. pepper
⅛ tsp. dried whole thyme
3 small new potatoes, peeled and cut into eighths
3 small carrots, pared and cut into 1 inch pieces
1 small onion coarsely chopped
1 stalk celery, sliced
½ cup frozen English peas

Coat lamb with flour and brown in hot oil in a Dutch oven. Add tomato, water and seasonings; cover and simmer over low heat 1 hour or until lamb is almost tender, stirring occasionally. Stir in vegetables except peas; cover and cook 30 minutes. Add peas; cover and cook 15 minutes stirring occasionally.

CRUSTY FRENCH LOAVES

1 cup plus 2 Tbsp. warm water (105° to 115°), divided
1 tsp. sugar
1 pkg. dry yeast
1 Tbsp. sugar

1 Tbsp. butter, melted
1 tsp. salt
3 to 3½ cups all-purpose flour, divided

Combine ¼ cup water, sugar and yeast; let stand 5 minutes. Combine remaining water, sugar, butter, salt and 1 cup flour in a large bowl; mix well. Stir in yeast mixture and enough of remaining flour to make a soft dough.

Turn dough out onto a floured surface and knead until smooth and elastic, about 5 minutes. Place in a well greased bowl, turning to grease top. Cover and let rise in a warm place, free from drafts, 1 hour or until doubled in bulk.

Punch dough down and divide into fourths. Shape each fourth into a ball and place on well greased baking sheets.
Make intersecting slits about ¼-inch deep across top of loaves with a sharp knife. Cover and let rise in a warm place, free from drafts, until doubled in bulk, about 40 minutes.

Place a pan of boiling water on lower rack of oven to obtain steam. Bake loaves at 400° for 15 to 20 minutes or until golden brown. Slice tops from crusty French loaves. Hollow out center of loaves leaving a ¾-inch thick shell. Spoon stew into bread shells and replace tops of loaves, slightly off center.

Sue Stacy

Seafood

BAIHIAN HALIBUT

2 Tbsp. extra virgin olive oil
2 Tbsp. fresh lime juice
4- 1 in. thick halibut steak halves (about 2 lbs.)
1 small onion, chopped
1 cup bell pepper, chopped
1 tsp. salt
2 large garlic cloves, thinly sliced
1 Serrano chili or jalapeño pepper, seeded and minced (include seeds for more heat)
½ cup unsweetened coconut milk
1 medium tomato, diced

With a fork, whisk 1 tablespoon of the oil and lime juice on large platter, add fish and turn to coat.

Heat remaining tablespoon oil in a 12-inch nonstick skillet over medium heat. Add onion and pepper. Cook 6 minutes until onion is translucent and pepper is just tender.

Sprinkle ½ teaspoon of the salt over fish. Add fish to skillet; pour coconut milk over fish and add tomato. Reduce heat to medium-low and simmer 8 to 9 minutes, turning fish halfway through cooking time. Stir remaining salt into sauce, spoon over fish a few times, and serve immediately.

Sue Stacy

BARBECUE SHRIMP WITH JAMBALAYA RICE

2 lb. raw shrimp, peeled
Louisiana barbeque seasoning
4 Tbsp. butter
½ cup trinity mix (prepackaged diced onions, peppers and celery)
2 andouille sausages, cut into bite-sized pieces
2 cups water
1- 5.7 oz. dirty rice mix
3 Tbsp. diced pimentos
5 garlic cloves, crushed
2 tsp. rosemary, chopped
1 Tbsp. Worcestershire sauce,
½ cup white wine,
1 tsp. pepper and
1½ tsp. hot pepper sauce (optional)

Heat saucepan for 3 minutes then add 1 tablespoon of butter and swirl it around until bottom is coated. Add the trinity mix and cook for 2 to 3 minutes or until tender. Add sausage along with water, rice mix and pimentos to pan while bringing it to a boil. Once boiling, turn down heat to low and cover, cooking for 6 to 7 minutes. Stir every so often. Let stand for 5 minutes and add parsley.

While rice is cooking, sprinkle Louisiana barbeque seasoning on shrimp. Heat a sauté pan for a few minutes and add 3 tablespoons butter. Swirl around while crushing garlic into pan. Cook garlic for 2 minutes. Put shrimp in pan for 3 to 4 minutes. Keep turning shrimp over until all become pink. Remove shrimp to a separate plate. Add rosemary, Worcestershire sauce, wine, pepper and hot pepper sauce to sauté pan. Cook for 2 to 3 minutes and or until liquid is about half of starting amount. Pour over shrimp.

Either serve shrimp separate from jambalaya rice or combine the two. I usually add it to jambalaya and like it to be more of a soup. I will often also add crawfish to soup when I add sausage and dirty rice.

Mark Thessin

LOW COUNTRY BOIL

This is an easy recipe and a favorite of the family.

Old Bay seasoning
Red potatoes
Sausage
Corn on the cob
Crab legs
Shrimp
Mussels (optional)

Heat a large pot of water and bring to a boil. This pot has to be rather large because of crab legs. Add Old Bay seasoning while water is boiling. I am rather liberal in how much I put in but don't overdo it depending on how much spice you want. Add several pounds of red potatoes depending on how many are being served. A good measure is ⅓- ½ pound per person. Also add two 16-ounce sausages cut up into 1-inch pieces. I usually split the sausages, one spicy and one normal. Cook potatoes and sausage for 10 minutes.

Add 1 ear of corn per person (husks and silk removed) and crab legs to pot. I use the rule of 1 cluster of crab legs, about 4 legs plus claw leg, per person. Cook for another 5 minutes. Note that at each step you are leaving everything previously cooked in the pot. Add shrimp to pot. I usually put ½ pound of shrimp per person. I also add mussels to the pot at this time but this is a personal preference. Cook for 3 minutes. Make sure you don't overcook this stage.

Mark Thessin

ORANGE ROUGHY IN SCALLION AND GINGER SAUCE

⅓ cup dry sherry
3 Tbsp. low-sodium soy sauce
2 tsp. sesame oil
¼ cup green onion, finely chopped
1 tsp. ginger, freshly grated
1 tsp. garlic, finely chopped
2 orange roughy fillets (1 pound)

Preheat the oven to 400°. Mix the sherry, soy sauce, sesame oil, onion, ginger and garlic in a small bowl. Place the fish fillets in an ovenproof casserole dish. Drizzle the marinade over the fish and bake for 12 minutes or until the fish flakes.

Sue Stacy

SALMON FILLETS

4-6 salmon fillets
⅛ tsp. salt
⅛ tsp. pepper
2 Tbsp. butter or olive oil
1½ Tbsp. honey
2 Tbsp. Dijon mustard
¼ cup bread crumbs
¼ cup, pecans, chopped
2 tsp. parsley, chopped

Sprinkle fillets with salt and pepper. Combine melted butter or olive oil with mustard and honey. Brush on fillets. Combine bread crumbs, pecans and parsley. Spread over fillets that have been placed in a 13 x 9-inch greased pan with skin side down. Bake at 450° for 10 to 15 minutes or until salmon flakes.

Jean Berry

SALMON BURGERS

1-14.75 oz. can salmon, drained and flaked
½ cup whole wheat bread or panka bread crumbs
½ cup onion, chopped
1 tsp. lemon juice
½ cup red bell pepper, chopped
1 Tbsp. lemon or orange peel
1 egg, slightly beaten
½ tsp. rosemary
½ tsp. pepper
Dash paprika
Several turns of freshly ground black pepper
3 Tbsp. vegetable oil

In a large bowl, gently mix together all ingredients except oil. Form into 8 patties, each about ½ inch thick. Heat oil over medium high heat in a large skillet. Cook the patties until nicely browned on both sides, about 3 to 4 minutes per side.

Kay Dozier

BROWN SUGAR-GLAZED SALMON

4 2-inch wide salmon fillets (1½ lbs. total)
¼ cup packed dark-brown sugar
2 tsp. butter
2 tsp. Dijon mustard
¼ tsp. each salt and pepper
8 oz. steamed snow peas
2 cups heat-and-serve brown rice

Heat oven to 325°. Line a small baking sheet with nonstick aluminum foil. Place salmon on sheet. In a small bowl, stir together brown sugar, butter, mustard, salt and pepper. Carefully spread over salmon pieces, dividing equally. Transfer salmon to oven and bake for 25 minutes, or until fish flakes easily with a fork. Serve with peas and rice.

Sharon Wilson

SESAME-CRUSTED SALMON WITH HONEY-GINGER VINAIGRETTE

This recipe may appear complicated but it is amazingly easy and delicious

2 large English cucumbers
½ cup rice wine vinegar
⅛ tsp. salt
2 Tbsp. sugar
¼ cup water
4- 4 oz. salmon filets
¼ cup soy sauce
2 Tbsp. rice wine vinegar
1 Tbsp. honey
1 pinch cayenne pepper
½ tsp. ground coriander
½ tsp. dark sesame oil
Sesame seeds

Peel and coarsely chop 1 cucumber; process in food processor until smooth. Strain, discarding pulp. Stir in rice wine vinegar and salt. Set aside. Combine sugar and water in a small saucepan and cook over medium heat until mixture boils. Stir into cucumber mixture. Combine soy sauce, vinegar honey pepper, coriander and sesame oil. Set aside.

Place salmon in a lightly greased baking pan. Brush soy sauce mixture over salmon. Sprinkle with sesame seeds. Bake at 450° for 10 to 12 minutes or until fish flakes.
Slice second cucumber into four pasta-style bowls. Place salmon on top of cucumbers. Spoon cucumber liquid mixture evenly into each dish. Drizzle with a small amount of Honey-Ginger Vinaigrette (for recipe see p. 69).

Gwen Perkins, Chapman's II

SALMON IN A BUNDLE

One each red, yellow and green bell pepper, sliced in strips
1 or 2 cups sugar snap peas
2 Tbsp. Sauvignon wine
2 Tbsp. extra virgin olive oil
Zest of 1 lemon
Juice of ½ lemon
2 slices lemon per piece of salmon
2 Tbsp. dried Thyme leaves
Kosher salt to taste
Cracked black pepper to taste
4 salmon steaks or straight cuts about 4 oz. each piece

Make a sheet of tin foil for each piece of salmon, approximately 12 inches long.

In a large mixing bowl, combine the peppers, peas, wine, zest, lemon juice and thyme leaves. Center a handful of the combined product on each piece of tin foil. Place a piece of salmon on top of each pepper bed; drizzle olive oil over the salmon. Sprinkle with salt and pepper.

Drizzle the remaining juices over the salmon pieces, then place 2 slices of lemon on each salmon piece. Close the tin foil to seal in the salmon completely and place the "bundles" on a cooking sheet. Preheat oven to 350°. Place cooking sheet in oven for 15 minutes. Remove and unwrap the salmon. Gingerly, slide the cooked vegetable and salmon onto your dinner plate.

Serve with a side dish of rice with golden raisins and chilled Chardonnay.

Bill Kennedy

SHRIMP AND GRITS

4 servings instant grits
2 Tbsp. extra virgin olive oil
1 medium onion
1 garlic clove, minced
1 lb. andouille sausage or Italian sausage, cut in chunks
¼ cup flour
2 cups chicken stock
2-3 bay leaves
2 lbs. shrimp, cleaned and deveined
Pinch cayenne pepper, to taste
Juice of ½ lemon
Ground black pepper
Green onions, sliced

Cook grits according to package directions and set aside.

Place a deep skillet over medium heat and coat with olive oil. Add the onion and garlic and sauté for 2 minutes. Add the sausage and cook till sausage is browned. Sprinkle flour and stir to create a roux. Slowly pour chicken stock, stirring to avoid lumps. Toss in the bay leaves until liquid comes to a simmer, then add shrimp. Poach shrimp for about 3 minutes. Add cayenne pepper and lemon juice. Season with black pepper and add green onions.

Spoon grits into a bowl and add the shrimp mixture.

Linda Green

TILAPIA WITH FLORENTINE ALFREDO PASTA

This was a favorite of Father Arnold's. It was always a pleasure cooking for him because I knew how much he appreciated it.

1 tsp. salt
5 tsp. flour
Tilapia
3 Tbsp. butter
¼ cup white wine
Juice of 1 lemon
5 sprigs parsley, chopped

Mix together salt and 4 teaspoons of flour in Ziploc bag. One at a time, place tilapia fillets in bag and shake until coated.

Heat frying pan for 2 to 3 minutes and once heated add 1 tablespoon of butter. Add another tablespoon of butter and place fish on top. Turn fish while making sure butter is always under fish. Cook 3 minutes or more or until fish is golden brown and flakes easily. Move fish to plate once done. Add ¼ cup of white wine to sauce pan, along with 1 tablespoon of butter, 1 teaspoon of flour and lemon juice. Heat another 1 to 2 minutes or until thickened. Add 5 sprigs of parsley chopped up. Pour over tilapia.

FLORENTINE PASTA
Fettuccine noodles
1-10 oz. box frozen spinach
1-16 oz. jar Alfredo sauce

Fill saucepan ½ full of water and bring to boil. Add fettuccine noodles and boil for 8 to 10 minutes while stirring occasionally. Remove spinach from box, place in a bowl and microwave for 5 to 7 minutes on high. After this stir in a 16 oz. jar of Alfredo sauce and microwave for 2 more minutes or until totally heated. Stir in drained pasta with Alfredo sauce and spinach and serve with tilapia dish.

Mark Thessin

Desserts

AUNT BETTY'S PEANUT BUTTER BALLS WITH CHOCOLATE DIP

A Christmas tradition. Aunt Betty makes and brings them to our Christmas Day celebration.

2 cups peanut butter (Aunt Betty likes Jif Smooth)
¾ cup margarine
1-16 oz. box powdered sugar
1 Tbsp. vanilla
⅓ bar paraffin wax
6 oz. semi-sweet chocolate morsels

Mix peanut butter, margarine, powdered sugar and vanilla and shape into 1-inch balls. Place on wax paper on cookie sheet. Chill in refrigerator for 30 to 45 minutes. Melt paraffin in double boiler. Add chocolate morsels and melt. Keep on warm. Dip peanut ball in chocolate and put on wax paper or cookie sheet to set. Can be refrigerated.

Marge Ellis

AMISH APPLE PIE

This is a family favorite and has been passed along to many friends – to become a favorite in their homes as well.

STREUSEL
⅓ cup granulated sugar
¼ cup brown sugar
½ cup plus 2 Tbsp. flour
1 tsp. cinnamon
1 tsp. nutmeg
Speck of salt
1 stick butter, cold
½ cup English walnuts, coarsely chopped

PIE
4 med. Granny Smith or McIntosh apples, sliced thin (4 cups)
1 unbaked 10-inch pie shell
1 cup sugar
3 Tbsp. flour
½ tsp. cinnamon
1 egg
1 cup heavy whipping cream
1 tsp. vanilla extract

In a food processor bowl, mix the first 6 streusel ingredients. Add the butter and process until the mixture is crumbly; it should still have a dry look to it – don't overprocess. Add the nuts, then set aside.

Preheat oven to 350°. Peel, core and thinly slice the apples; there should be 4 cups. Place the apples in the pie shell. In a small bowl, mix the sugar, flour and cinnamon. Beat the egg in a medium bowl, and add the cream and vanilla. Add the sugar mixture to the egg mixture and blend. Pour over the apples. Bake for 1 hour in the lower one-third of the oven. After 20 minutes, sprinkle streusel over the top and continue baking approximately 40 minutes longer, or until the top puffs and is golden brown.

Jeannette Teague

APPLE BETTY PIE

A family favorite for years!

4 cups tart apples, sliced and pared
¼ cup orange juice
1 cup sugar
¾ cup all-purpose flour
½ tsp. cinnamon
¼ tsp. nutmeg
¼ tsp. ground cloves
Dash of salt
½ cup butter

Mound apples in buttered 9-inch pie pan; sprinkle with orange juice. For topping combine sugar, flour, spices and a dash of salt; cut in butter until mixture is crumbly; then scatter over apples. Bake at 375° for 45 minutes or until apples are done and topping is crisp. Serve with vanilla ice cream.

Peggy Killmeyer

APRICOT NECTAR CAKE

CAKE
1 package Duncan Hines Lemon Supreme cake mix
½ cup sugar
¾ cup oil
1 cup apricot nectar
4 eggs

GLAZE
1 box confectioners' sugar
2 Tbsp. lemon juice
Enough apricot nectar to make this glaze pourable

Mix all, adding eggs one at a time. Pour into a Bundt pan which has been greased and floured. Bake at 350° for 45 to 55 minutes (until tester comes out clean). Cool and remove from pan by inverting on cake plate. Spoon or drizzle glaze over. If there is extra glaze, pour it in the center.

Sue Stacy

NO-BAKE APPLE PIE

5 medium tart apples, peeled and sliced (I used Macintosh)
1¾ cups water, divided
1-.3 oz. pkg. sugar-free lemon gelatin (Jell-o)
½ teaspoon ground cinnamon
¼ teaspoon ground nutmeg
1-.8 oz. pkg. sugar-free cook-and-serve vanilla pudding mix (I used instant)
½ cup pecans, chopped
1-9 in. reduced-fat graham cracker crust (or regular graham crackers)
½ cup fat-free whipped topping

In a large saucepan, combine the sliced apples, 1 cup water, gelatin, cinnamon and nutmeg. Bring to boil. Reduce heat, cover and simmer for 6 minutes or until apples are tender.

Combine the dry pudding mix and remaining water; add to apple mixture. Cook for 1 minute or until thickened. Remove from the heat; stir in nuts.

Pour into the crust. Refrigerate for at least 2 hours before serving. Garnish with whipped topping.

Kay Dozier

BISHOP WHIPPLE'S PUDDING

Some dear friends served this dessert to my husband and I the first time we were invited to their home in 1975. It is unique as well as delicious!

1 Tbsp. unsalted butter, softened
2 eggs
½ cup sugar
2/3 cup all-purpose flour
1 tsp. baking powder
½ tsp. vanilla extract
1 cup pecans, coarsely chopped
1 cup pitted dates, coarsely chopped
1 cup heavy cream, chilled
2 Tbsp. dry sherry (optional)

Preheat oven to 350°. Brush bottom and sides of a one quart soufflé or baking dish with the butter and set aside.

In a large mixing bowl, beat eggs with a wire whisk or electric beater until frothy. Beat in sugar, flour and baking powder. Add vanilla, nuts and dates and continue beating until ingredients are well combined. Pour into prepared dish and bake in the center of the oven for 25 minutes or until the pudding no longer wobbles. Cool 15 minutes.

Whip the cream until it forms soft peaks. Gently add sherry if desired. I do not typically add the sherry. Instead, I fold a little sugar into the cream. Scoop pudding into small bowls or onto dessert plates and add dollops of whipped cream. Bring the whipped cream to the table so guests can add more if desired.

Sue Stacy

CARROT CAKE WITH CREAM CHEESE FROSTING

4 eggs
2 cups sugar
1½ cup oil
3 small jars strained carrots
1 small can pineapple tidbits, drained
1 cup nuts, chopped
1 cup raisins
2 cups flour
1 tsp. salt
2 tsp. baking soda
2 tsp. cinnamon
1 tsp. vanilla

Mix eggs and sugar well. Add next 5 ingredients. Add the dry ingredients. Blend in the cinnamon and vanilla. Bake in a 13-inch rectangular pan that has been greased, at 375° for 50 to 55 minutes or until done.

CREAM CHEESE FROSTING
½ stick butter
½ box confectioners' sugar
1 tsp. vanilla
4 oz. cream cheese

Blend together butter and cheese then add sugar and vanilla. Sprinkle chopped nuts on top if desired

Ruth Ann Graveno

CHUNKY APPLE WALNUT CAKE

1½ cup vegetable oil
2 cups sugar
3 eggs
2 cups all-purpose flour, sifted
⅛ tsp. ground cloves
1¼ tsp. ground cinnamon
¼ tsp. ground mace
1 tsp. baking soda
¾ tsp. salt
1 cup whole wheat flour, sifted
1¼ cup walnuts chopped
3¼ cup Rome Beauty apples, peeled and chopped
3 Tbsp. calvados (apple brandy)

Preheat oven to 325°. In a large bowl, beat oil and sugar until thick and opaque. Add eggs one at a time beating well after each addition. Sift together flour, cloves cinnamon, mace, baking soda and salt. Then stir in whole wheat flour.

Add to liquid mixture until well blended. Add walnuts, apple chunks and Calvados all at once and stir. Pour batter into greased 10-inch round baking pan. Bake for 1 hour, 15 minutes or until cake tester comes out clean. Let cake rest for 10 minutes, then unmold.

Terry Bies

BARB'S CHOCOLATE CAKE

3 cups packed light brown sugar (I often mix light and dark brown sugar half and half)
1 cup butter, softened (do not substitute margarine)
4 large eggs
2 tsp. vanilla extract
2 2/3 cup all-purpose flour (I use cake flour)
¾ cup baking cocoa (I use half dark chocolate cocoa, half regular cocoa)
1 Tbsp. baking soda
½ teaspoon salt
1⅓ cup sour cream (don't use light or fat free)
1⅓ cup boiling water

Preheat oven to 350°. Grease and flour four 9-inch round cake pans. In a large mixing bowl, cream brown sugar and butter. Add eggs, one at a time, beating well after each addition. Beat on high speed of electric mixer until light and fluffy. Blend in vanilla. In another mixing bowl, combine flour, cocoa, baking soda and salt; add alternately (begin and end with flour mixture) with sour cream to creamed mixture (will be thick). Mix on low speed just until combined. Stir in boiling water just until blended (batter will be thin). Pour into prepared cake pans. Bake for 25 to 30 minutes or until center tests done with a toothpick. Cool in pans 10 minutes. Remove to wire rack to cool completely.

FROSTING
½ cup butter (do not substitute margarine)
3-1 oz. squares unsweetened chocolate
3-1 oz. squares semisweet chocolate
5 cup confectioners' sugar
1 cup sour cream (not light or fat free)
2 tsp. vanilla extract

In a medium saucepan, melt butter and chocolate over low heat, stirring constantly to prevent burning. Cool several minutes. In a mixing bowl, combine sugar, sour cream and vanilla. Add chocolate mixture and beat with an electric mixer until smooth. Frost cooled cake. Store in an airtight container. (I normally have the cake on a plate and use a cake cover – it is not airtight – but I do refrigerate the cake if I am keeping it for a couple of days. It is best if served at room temp. It will be moister after a day or so.) This cake can be frozen either whole or in sections. I often cut it in quarters and wrap each separately, so I can take out only one section when I need it and not have to thaw the whole cake.

Jeanette Teague

CHOCOLATE PEANUT CANDY

1 pkg. vanilla or chocolate bark (but use only 8 squares of 12 in pkg. for this recipe)
1 cup crunchy peanut butter
1 cup Rice Krispies
2 cups mini marshmallows

Melt bark in double boiler until smooth. Add peanut butter and Rice Krispies. Stir until mixed. Cool for about 10 minutes before adding marshmallows. If too warm the marshmallows will melt and they should be whole. When cool enough but still warm add the marshmallows, mixing them in. Drop by teaspoonful onto cookie sheet covered with wax paper. Cool for about 15 minutes. Done!

Diane Serfass

COCONUT POUND CAKE

1 cup Crisco shortening
2 cups sugar
6 eggs
2 cups flour
2 tsp. baking powder
¼ tsp. salt
1 cup buttermilk

1- 4 oz. can flaked coconut
1 tsp. vanilla
1 tsp. coconut flavoring
1 cup sugar
1 tsp. coconut flavoring
1 cup water

Cream Crisco and sugar. Add eggs one at a time. Add dry ingredients alternately with buttermilk. Add vanilla, coconut and coconut flavoring. Bake in a greased and floured Bundt pan at 350° for 50 minutes to 1 hour. Mix sugar and water together in a small saucepan. Bring to a boil; boil 1 minute. Add coconut flavoring. Brush on cake while still hot.

Jean M. Berry

CHERRY DELIGHT

36 soda crackers
1½ cup sugar
1 cup nuts
1 tsp. vanilla
5 egg whites, beaten stiff
1 pkg. Dream Whip or Cool Whip
1 sm. can crushed pineapple, drained
Maraschino cherries

Mix all ingredients together and spread into a well-buttered dish. Bake at 325° for 35 minutes. Cool. Mix Dream Whip or Cool Whip and cover mixture. Add crushed pineapple and maraschino cherries.

Kitty McNally

RICH CHOCOLATE CAKE

1 pkg. German chocolate cake mix
1- 4 oz. pkg. instant chocolate pudding mix
16 oz. sour cream
4 eggs
½ cup Kahlua liqueur
¾ cup oil
12 oz. chocolate chips

Mix all ingredients. Bake in greased and floured Bundt pan at 350° for 50 to 60 minutes. Cake is done when you shake it and it doesn't move. This cake needs no frosting; it is very moist.

Nancy Tuberty

COCONUT CRUNCH DELIGHT

½ cup butter or margarine, melted
1 cup all-purpose flour
1¼ cup flaked coconut
¼ cup packed brown sugar
1 cup slivered almonds
1- 3.4 oz. pkg. instant vanilla pudding mix
1- 3.4 oz. pkg. instant coconut cream pudding mix
2-2/3 cups cold milk
2 cups whipped topping
Fresh strawberries, optional

In a bowl, combine the first five ingredients; press lightly into a greased 13 x 9 x 2-inch baking pan. Bake at 350° for 25 to 30 minutes or until golden brown, stirring every 10 minutes to form coarse crumbs. Cool. Divide crumb mixture in half; press half into the same baking pan. In a mixing bowl, beat pudding mixes and milk. Fold in whipped topping; spoon over the crust. Top with remaining crumb mixture. Cover and refrigerate overnight. Garnish with strawberries if desired.

Cory McCormick

COCONUT-ALMOND MACAROONS

3 Tbsp. almond paste
1 tsp. vanilla extract
4 large egg whites, divided
1⅓ cups powdered sugar
1¼ tsp. baking powder
¼ tsp. salt
3½ cups flaked sweetened coconut
½ cup granulated sugar

Preheat oven to 350°. Combine almond paste, vanilla and 2 egg whites in a large bowl; beat with a mixer until well blended.

Combine powdered sugar, baking powder and salt. Add powdered sugar mixture to almond paste mixture, beating until blended. Stir in coconut. Place remaining 2 egg whites in a medium bowl; beat with a mixer at high speed until soft peaks form using clean, dry beaters. Gradually add granulated sugar, 1 tablespoon at a time, beating until stiff peaks form. Gently fold egg white mixture into coconut mixture. Drop dough by level tablespoons 2 inches apart onto baking sheets lined with parchment paper.

Bake for 17 minutes or until firm. Cool on pans 2 to 3 minutes on a wire rack. Remove cookies from pan, and cool completely on wire rack.

Diane Marek

FROZEN STRAWBERRY DESSERT

1- 10 oz. pkg. frozen strawberries or 2 boxes fresh strawberries
1 cup sugar
1 cup sour cream
1 tsp. vanilla

Blend and freeze. May be frozen in parfait glasses.

Judy Tajague

CRANBERRY WALNUT TORTE
A great dessert during the holidays

⅓ cup margarine
3 Tbsp. sugar
1 egg
1 cup flour
¼ tsp. salt
1½ cup whole cranberries
¾ cup walnut
2 eggs
2/3 cup light corn syrup
¼ cup sugar
1 Tbsp. margarine, melted

Mix the margarine, sugar, egg, flour and salt together. Press the mixture into the bottom of 9-inch springform pan, forming a 1-inch edge up the sides of pan. Sprinkle cranberries and walnuts over the top of crust. Then, blend together the eggs, corn syrup, sugar and margarine and pour over the cranberries and walnuts. Bake at 350° for 1 hour until center is almost set. Serve at room temperature with ice cream if desired. Refrigerate leftovers.

Sheri Isham

DELICIOUS HOMEMADE HOT FUDGE

1 stick margarine
4–5 Tbsp. cocoa
1 small can evaporated milk
2 cups powdered sugar

Melt margarine and then add evaporated milk, powdered sugar and cocoa. Bring mixture to a boil and boil over medium heat for 5 minutes, stirring constantly. Allow to slightly cool. Serve over ice cream and enjoy. Remaining fudge can be refrigerated and later reheated in the microwave.

Sheri Isham

Two great cooks submitted different easy peach cobbler recipes. You can decide which is best—and easiest!

EASY PEACH COBBLER I

3 cup peaches, sliced
1 tsp. lemon juice
½ tsp. nutmeg
½ tsp. cinnamon
1 cup self-rising flour
1 egg beaten
1 cup sugar
1 stick butter, melted

Place peaches in baking dish. Sprinkle with lemon juice, cinnamon and nutmeg. Mix flour, egg and sugar to crumb texture. Sprinkle over peaches. Pour melted butter evenly over the mixture. Bake at 350° for 30 to 35 minutes.

Carole Guthrie

EASY PEACH COBBLER II

1 stick unsalted butter or margarine, melted
1- 29 oz. can peaches, drained
1- 21 oz. can peach pie filling
¾ cup pecans, chopped
½ cup lemon juice
1 box yellow cake mix

Cut drained peach slices in half, if desired. Add to peach pie filling with lemon juice. Spread this mixture in the bottom of 9 x 13 x 2-inch baking pan. Mix together cake mix, pecans and butter (mixture will be crumbly). Spread this mixture over the peach mixture already in the baking pan. Bake uncovered at 350° for 45 minutes. Serve warm with vanilla ice cream, if desired.

Sue Kelley

EASY CARAMEL ROLLS

16 Rhodes frozen rolls
1 pkg. butterscotch pudding (not instant)
½ cup brown sugar
6 Tbsp. margarine

The night before, place 16 frozen rolls in 9 x 13-inch pan. Sprinkle the butterscotch pudding over the rolls. Melt brown sugar and margarine. Drizzle the brown sugar/margarine mixture over the rolls. Cover with plastic wrap and let sit over night. In the morning remove plastic wrap and bake at 350° for approximately 15 minutes.

Sheri Isham

FROZEN CHOCOLATE MOUSSE

¾ pkg. Oreo cookies, crushed
12 oz. package chocolate chips
½ cup water
1 tsp. instant coffee
4 eggs, separated
½ cup sugar
3 cups whipping cream
5 Tbsp. powdered sugar
1 tsp. vanilla

Prepare crust by pressing on the bottom of a 9-inch springform pan. Boil water. Stir in coffee and chocolate chips until melted. Whip egg whites with sugar until soft peaks form. Whip egg yolks until lemon colored. Whip whipping cream. Add powdered sugar and vanilla by gently folding into whipped cream.

Fold melted and cooled chocolate mixture with egg yolks. Fold egg whites to mixture. Fold whipping cream to entire mixture. Gently spoon mixture into prepared springform pan. Freeze overnight. Serve when slightly thawed.

Lucy Quillin

ÉCLAIR CAKE

COCOA TOPPING
1 stick margarine
¼ cup milk
1 cup sugar
½ tsp. vanilla
⅓ cup cocoa
⅛ tsp. salt

BOTTOM
Graham crackers

PUDDING BATTER
2 regular boxes instant vanilla pudding
3 cups milk
8 oz. Cool Whip topping

Melt margarine in a medium sauce pan. Add sugar, cocoa and milk. Bring to a boil and cook for one minute. Remove from heat. Add vanilla and salt. Set aside.

Mix pudding mix and milk, fold in Cool Whip. Set aside.

In a 9 x 13-inch pan, layer whole Graham crackers to cover bottom of pan. Spread half the pudding mixture. Layer a second layer of Graham crackers, spread other half of pudding. Put on 3rd layer of Graham crackers and spread cocoa topping over Graham cracker layer. Refrigerate at least 3 to 4 hours.

Nena Manci

FLAN NAPOLITANO

4 eggs
1 can sweetened condensed milk
1 can evaporated milk
4 Tbsp. sugar
¼ tsp. vanilla
1- 3 cup round mold with tight lid, making sure you have 2nd larger mold to insert this mold with 1 inch hot water if method 2 is chosen.

Pour sugar in the container and bake over medium heat, until sugar melts and becomes golden brown, or caramelized. Once melted remove from oven and quickly tilt mold to coat bottom and sides. In blender or mixer pour eggs, condensed milk, evaporated milk and vanilla, mix well. Pour mixture into caramel-coated mold.

There are 2 ways to proceed from here:

Method 1: Set the mold in pressure cooker with water (about 1 inch in depth), making sure the lid is tight so that the water in the pressure cooker does not get into the flan. Cook for about 35 minutes in medium heat, when pressure cooker sounds, leave another 5 minutes, remove from heat and let cool. Remove the flan and chill. Carefully loosen custard from sides and center; invert on platter.

Method 2: Set the mold in baking pan on oven rack. Pour hot water in the baking pan to a depth of 1 inch. Bake, uncovered, in 325° oven for 50 to 55 minutes or till a knife inserted halfway between center and edge comes out clean. Chill. Carefully loosen custard from sides and center; invert on platter.

Blanca Scott

GINGERBREAD BOY COOKIES

2 cups packed brown sugar
1½ cups butter, softened
1 egg
2 tsp. ground cinnamon
1 tsp. ground nutmeg
½ tsp. ground cloves
¼ tsp. baking soda
4 cups flour

Cream together sugar, butter and egg until fluffy. Add remaining ingredients. Mix well, chill 2 hours. Roll on lightly floured surface to ⅛ inch thickness. Cut with small gingerbread boy cutter. Place on greased cookie sheet and bake at 350° for 8 to 10 minutes.

Cory McCormick

GOLDEN ORANGE DREAMSICLE CAKE

CAKE
1 box orange supreme cake Mix
1½ cup milk
½ cup oil
1 small box instant vanilla pudding
1 small box orange Jell-o
4 eggs

Combine all ingredients in mixer bowl; Beat 3 minutes and pour into 3- 9- inch cake pans. Bake at 350 ° for 25 minutes or till done. Cool completely then fill between layers with filling and then with frosting (below).

FILLING
8 oz. sour cream
1 medium can crushed pineapple, drained
2 cups sugar
8-12 oz. frozen grated coconut

Mix together; reserve 1 cup filling. Fill between layers on cooled cake.

FROSTING
8 oz. Cool Whip

Mix reserved cup of filling with Cool Whip. Frost top and sides of cake and refrigerate for about 48 hours before serving to allow flavors to marry.

Pam Lewis

HEAVENLY HASH

These make great Christmas gifts!

1- 12 oz. Hershey Silver Bells
1- 12 oz. Hershey Almond Chocolates
1 small bag miniature marshmallows
½ cup pecans, chopped

In a Pyrex bowl melt chocolates in microwave oven on low heat. With a spatula mix chocolate every few minutes until chocolate is completely melted. Then add pecans and marshmallows and mix well. Pour mixture into a small baking pan lined with foil. Refrigerate until hard. Cut into squares.

Judy Tujague

HOLIDAY PIE

This is always a BIG hit.

1-10 inch unbaked pie crust
½ cup all-purpose flour
1¼ cup sugar
1 tsp. cinnamon
1-12 oz. bag fresh cranberries
2 or 3 Granny Smith apples, peeled, cored and chopped (about 2¾ cups)
¼ cup sugar
⅓ cup butter, cut into small pieces

Adjust oven rack to lowest level. Preheat oven to 425°. In a large bowl combine flour, sugar and cinnamon. Rinse and remove any stems and spoiled cranberries and drain well. Add cranberries and apples to sugar mixture stir to mix well. Pour fruits into unbaked pie shell. Combine flour, sugar and butter in a small bowl. Blend with a fork or pastry blender until crumbly. Sprinkle over filling.
Bake in oven 15 minutes. Reduce heat to 350° and continue baking 35 to 45 minutes or until crust and topping are lightly browned. Cool before serving.

Pat Zeber

JEFF'S COOKIES

This is my husband's favorite cookie.

2 cups butter, softened
1 cup sugar
1 cup light brown sugar, packed
2 large eggs
2 tsp. vanilla
4 cups flour
1 tsp. baking soda
12 oz. chocolate chips
12 oz. peanut butter chips
1 cup salted peanuts
2 cups pretzels

Preheat oven 350°. In a large bowl cream butter and sugar until light and fluffy. Beat in eggs and vanilla. Combine dry ingredients. Stir in chips, peanuts and pretzels. Drop by heaping tablespoons on ungreased sheets. Bake 10 to 13 minutes. Do not overbake. Cool 1 minute on sheet.

Marlene Johnson

LEMON CHEESE TORTE

8 egg whites
1 Tbsp. white vinegar
2 cups sugar
2 cans sweetened condensed milk
2 -8 oz. pkg. cream cheese
1 cup fresh squeezed lemon juice, about 5-6 lemons
2 Tbsp. lemon rind, grated
1 container Cool Whip

Preheat oven to 300°. Beat egg whites until foamy. Add vinegar and beat until soft peaks form. Gradually add sugar and beat 8 minutes more until stiff. Evenly spread in a lightly greased 9 x 13 inch pan or two 8 x 8-inch pans. Bake for 1 hour.

Remove from oven and let the shell cool Use a fork to press down the egg white crust, leaving an edge to surround the filling. Use mixer to mix softened cream cheese until creamy. Add the 2 cans of condensed milk and blend. Add the cup of lemon juice and grated rind and blend well. Pour into the shells. Spread a layer of Cool Whip over the top. Optional: sprinkle a bit of grated lemon rind or nutmeg for color or nutmeg.

Mary Ann Thompson

LEMON SPONGE PUDDING

¼ cup flour
¼ tsp. salt
¾ cup sugar
2 Tbsp. butter
3 egg yolks

2 Tbsp. grated lemon rind
1 cup milk
¼ cup lemon juice
3 egg whites

Beat egg whites and set aside. Cream sugar and butter until blended. Next, beat in egg yolks and rind. Add dry ingredients alternately with liquids until blended. Gently fold in whites.

Pour into a greased, shallow casserole dish. Place this in a pan with 1 inch of hot water. Bake in a 350° oven for 50 to 60 minutes. This pudding has a cake-type top with a lemon custard sauce on the bottom. It goes well with blueberries and strawberries.

Anna Hannigan

LUSCIOUS LEMON RING

2 pkg. lemon pudding
1 cup sugar
1 envelope unflavored gelatin
1 angel food cake, cut into
bite-sized pieces
4 egg yolks

4 cups water
1 lemon rind, grated
1 cup heavy cream, whipped
1- 3½ oz. can coconut
Lemons

In saucepan, combine pudding, sugar and gelatin; stir in egg yolks and water. Mix well. Cook, stirring, over medium-high heat until boiling. Remove from heat and add lemon rind. Set saucepan into large bowl of ice cubes and cool 15 minutes. Butter or oil a 10-inch tube pan. When filling is cooled, fold in cream and coconut. Add cake cubes and mix. Put in pan and refrigerate covered overnight. Invert pan on serving dish. Decorate with cream, coconut and lemons.

Jeannette C. Spellman

MAMA'S SWEET SALTINES

After a meal, mama always says, "I need a little something sweet." Or salty – beware, they're addictive!

40 saltine crackers (Substitute graham crackers for a sweeter snack. I prefer graham crackers)
1 stick unsalted butter
1 cup light-brown sugar (organic is best)
8 oz. semisweet chocolate chips (about 1⅓ cups)

Preheat oven to 425°. Line a large rimmed cookie sheet with aluminum foil and crackers. In a medium pan, melt butter and brown sugar together and bring to a boil. Boil for 5 minutes, stirring regularly. Remove from heat and pour over crackers, covering them evenly. Put cookie sheet into oven and watch closely. Bake for about 5 minutes, or until just bubbly.

Remove from oven and pour chocolate chips over crackers. When chips begin to melt, spread them over crackers with a knife. Transfer pan to freezer for 15 to 20 minutes or until completely cold. The chocolate-covered crackers will form a solid sheet. Break into pieces and store in an airtight container.

Kay Dozier

OUTSTANDING FUDGE PIE

2 eggs
1½ cups sugar
3 Tbsp. cocoa
4 Tbsp. melted butter
½ cup evaporated milk
1 tsp. vanilla
1 unbaked pie crust

Mix all. Pour into crust. Bake in preheated 400° oven for 10 minutes. Reduce heat to 350° and bake 20 minutes longer. Cool completely.

Sue Stacy

MICROWAVE FUDGE
My favorite go-to treat recipe in the world...always a crowd pleaser!

1 lb. box powdered sugar
½ cup cocoa
¼ cup milk
1 stick butter
1 tsp. vanilla flavoring
¼ to ½ cup nuts (optional)

In a large microwave safe bowl stir together sugar and cocoa. Put milk and butter on top. Microwave on high 2 minutes. Remove and stir until smooth (Microwave in additional 30 second intervals if needed). When smooth, add 1 teaspoon vanilla and nuts if using. Pour into a greased 8 x 8-inch pan. Refrigerate 1 hour. HINT: Line the square pan with foil, then butter it. Lift the foil out when the fudge is set.

Claudia Finnegan

MY MOM'S OLD-FASHIONED RICE PUDDING
I love you, Mom!

1 qt. milk
¼ cup rice
¼ cup sugar
Pinch salt
Pinch butter
1 tsp. vanilla
Pinch nutmeg
½ pint cream

Mix together all ingredients except cream and bake at 350° for 1½ hours. Add ½ pint of cream and bake until creamy.

Pat Thompson

MOLASSES CAKE

This is also known as eggless and milkless cake

½ cup sugar
½ cup shortening
1 cup molasses
2½ cup flour
2 Tbsp. cocoa
1½ tsp. baking soda
½ tsp. salt
1 tsp. allspice
1 tsp. cinnamon
½ tsp. ground cloves
½ tsp. ground ginger
1 cup hot coffee

Cream sugar and shortening, add molasses. In a separate bowl, mix flour and remaining dry ingredients. Add flour mixture to molasses mixture and mix thoroughly, then add hot coffee a little at a time stirring constantly. Beat well. When completely mixed pour into a 9 x 13-inch greased pan.

The recipe is old and doesn't give amount of time or temperature. My guess is regular cake baking time 20 to 30 minutes and 350°. Remove when done (toothpick inserted come out clean) and let cool on cookie rack. The cake can be eaten plain, with a dusting of confectioners' sugar, with ice cream, or with icing. Nuts can also be added to this cake.

Yvette Woods

OATMEAL CAKE

1 cup oats
1¼ cup boiling water
½ cup butter
1 cup sugar
1 cup brown sugar
1 tsp. vanilla
2 eggs
1½ cup flour
½ tsp. salt
¾ tsp. cinnamon
¼ tsp. nutmeg
1 tsp. baking soda

Pour boiling water over oats and let stand 20 minutes. Mix butter, sugars, vanilla and eggs and add to oats. Sift flour, salt, cinnamon, nutmeg and baking soda and add to oat mixture. Pour into 8-inch pan and bake for 50 minutes at 350°.

Tracy Barnes

OATMEAL RAISIN COOKIES

These are crisp, yummy cookies and nobody eats just one! Bon Appétit!

1 cup shortening
1 cup white sugar
1 cup dark brown sugar
1 tsp. vanilla
2 eggs
1½ cups plain flour
1 tsp. salt
1 tsp. baking soda
3 cups old-fashioned oats
¾ cup raisins
¾ cup pecans

Cream shortening, sugars, vanilla and eggs. Add flour, salt and baking soda. Once these ingredients are combined, add oats, raisins and pecans. Roll into logs, slice and bake at 350° for 12 minutes.

Brenda Walsh

OATMEAL CHOCOLATE CHIP COOKIES

1½ cup sifted flour
¼ tsp. salt
1 cup shortening (I use unsalted butter)
½ cup brown sugar
½ cup white sugar
2 eggs
1 tsp. baking soda
1 cup pecans or walnuts, chopped (I toast the nuts in the oven for 2-3 minutes, this helps release flavors)
1- 12 oz. package semi-sweet chocolate chips
2 cups uncooked old-fashioned oatmeal
1 tsp. vanilla

Preheat oven to 350° or a convection oven at 325°. Sift together flour, soda and salt. Cream shortening (or butter), gradually adding the sugars, cream until light and fluffy. Add eggs one at a time, beating after each addition. Add dry ingredients and mix well. Stir in by hand the nuts, chips and oatmeal. Mix well and add the vanilla.

Drop cookie dough the size of a small egg onto greased cookie sheet. Bake 10 to 14 minutes or until browned.

These cookies will bake beautifully by using a convection oven. Co Bake until a golden brown. The top and bottom of the cookie will be the same exact color, light brown.

P.S. This cookie dough can be spooned into cookie shapes and placed in a covered 9 x 13-inch cake container to freeze. One can then take out a dozen frozen cookies and bake whenever you need fresh cookies. Bake at 350° degrees until browned.

Mary Ann Thompson

PEACH PIE
Delightful!

1 cup flour
1 stick butter
1 cup chopped & ground nuts
1-8 oz. pkg. cream cheese
¾ cup sugar
1½ cup water
4 Tbsp. cornstarch
1 cup sugar
4 Tbsp. peach Jell-o
5-6 cups fresh peaches, sliced

With a food processor grind the nuts, then add butter and flour. Blend ingredients until the dough forms a ball. Place dough into 9 x 13-inch cake pan and press dough up the sides with hands. Bake at 350° until lightly browned. Cool.

Cream sugar and cream cheese and spread on cooled crust. Mix water, cornstarch and sugar and cook until thickened, stirring constantly. Add Jell-o, continuing to stir. Cool. Add peaches. Refrigerate until cooled. Pour over the cream cheese and crust. Chill. Serve with Cool Whip, or whipped cream

Mary Ann Thompson

PECAN PIE BARS

1 cup flour
¼ cup sugar
Dash salt
6 Tbsp. butter
1 cup firmly packed brown sugar
1 cup light corn syrup
½ cup butter
4 large eggs, lightly beaten
2½ cups pecans, finely chopped
1 tsp. vanilla extract

Combine flour, sugar and salt in large bowl. Cut in ¾ cup butter thoroughly with a pastry blender until mixture resembles very fine crumbs. Press mixture evenly into a 9 x 13-inch pan. Bake at 350° for 17 to 20 minutes or until lightly browned.

Combine brown sugar, corn syrup and ½ cup butter in a sauce pan, bring to a boil over medium heat. Hold the boil for I minute, stirring gently. Remove from heat.

Stir in pecans and vanilla. Pour filling over crust. Bake at 350° for 34 to 35 min. or until set. Cool completely in pan on a wire rack. Cut into bars.

Rosemary Strawn

PECAN PIE

4 eggs, beaten separately
1 cup sugar
1 cup white Karo syrup
1 tsp. vanilla
2 Tbsp. butter
1 cup pecans

Cream egg yolks, add sugar, syrup, vanilla and blend well. Fold in well beaten egg whites. Pour mixture into a rich uncooked pastry shell. Bake in moderate oven until the consistency of custard pie, then cover top of pie thickly with halves of pecans and brown lightly.

Judy Tujague

PEITZELS

6 eggs
1 cup margarine, melted and cooled
1½ cup sugar
2 Tbsp. spoons anise seed
3½ cups flour
4 tsp. baking powder

Beat the eggs then add the sugar and beat until smooth. Add the cooled margarine and flavoring. Add the flour and baking powder. Drop about 1 teaspoon on the peitzel iron and press closed for about 1 minute. The first few may stick some. They should be a golden brown. Place on a rack to cool then place in an airtight tin to store.

Ruth Ann Graveno

PINEAPPLE AND MARSHMALLOW PUDDING

Delicious!

1 bag miniature marshmallow
1 Tbsp. vanilla
2 large cans crushed pineapple
1 Tbsp. sugar
2 pt. heavy whipping cream

One day before serving put marshmallows in extra-large bowl. Cover marshmallows with pineapple, then with a clean dish cloth. Let stand overnight.

The next day mix pineapple and marshmallows with mixer. In a separate (cold) bowl whip heavy whipping cream, vanilla and sugar, being careful not to over whip. Whipping cream should be just starting to form stiff peaks. Add to pineapple mix and beat some more.

Pudding will be lumpy. HINT: Putting the mixing bowl for the cream and the beaters in the fridge the night before will help whip the cream faster.

Yvette Woods

PUMPKIN POUND CAKE WITH BUTTERMILK GLAZE

CAKE
Cooking spray
1 Tbsp. all-purpose flour
1-15 oz. can pumpkin
¾ cup granulated sugar
¾ cup packed dark brown sugar
½ cup butter, softened
4 large eggs
1 tsp. vanilla extract
3 cups all-purpose flour
1½ tsp. pumpkin pie spice
1 tsp. baking powder
½ tsp. baking soda
½ tsp. salt
¾ cup fat-free buttermilk

GLAZE
⅓ cup fat-free buttermilk
¼ cup granulated sugar
2 Tbsp. butter
2 tsp. cornstarch
⅛ tsp. baking soda

Preheat oven to 350°. To prepare the cake, lightly coat a 10 inch tube pan with cooking spray; dust with 1 tablespoon flour. Spread pumpkin over 2 layers of paper towels; cover with 2 additional layers of paper towels. Let stand about 10 minutes. Scrape drained pumpkin into a bowl.

Place ¾ cup granulated sugar, brown sugar, and ½ cup butter in a large bowl; beat with a mixer at medium speed 3 minutes or until well blended. Add eggs, 1 at a time, beating well after each addition. Beat in pumpkin and vanilla. Lightly spoon 3 cups flour into dry measuring cups, and level with a knife. Combine flour and next 4 ingredients (through salt) in a bowl, stirring well with a whisk. Add flour mixture and ¾ cup buttermilk alternately to sugar mixture, beginning and ending with flour mixture.

Spoon batter into prepared pan. Bake at 350° for 55 minutes or until a wooden pick inserted in center comes out clean. Cool in pan 10 minutes on a wire rack. Remove from pan, and cool completely on wire rack.

To prepare glaze, combine ⅓ cup buttermilk and remaining ingredients in a small saucepan over medium heat; bring to a boil. Cook 1 minute or until thick, stirring constantly; remove from heat. Drizzle cake with glaze.

Karen Updike

PUMPKIN ROLL

This came from a dear friend of my mom's. We make it once a year either at Thanksgiving or Christmas. It is one of our very favorites. We always double it of course.

CAKE
3 eggs
1 cup sugar
2/3 cup pumpkin
¾ cup flour
1 tsp. baking soda
½ tsp. cinnamon
Chopped pecans (optional)
Powdered sugar

Mix all ingredients together very well. Pour mixture into a greased and wax-paper lined 10 x 15-inch cookie sheet. Sprinkle with chopped pecans if you like. Bake at 350° for 10 to15 minutes. Do not overbake. Turn onto a powdered sugared towel and roll up jelly-roll style until cool.

FILLING
1- 8 oz. bar of cream cheese
2 Tbsp. butter
¾ tsp. vanilla
1 cup powdered sugar

Beat until smooth. Spread on cake and roll it up. Refrigerate for 1 hour or freeze.

Erin Morel

RAW BROWNIE BITES

I recently was recommended these by a friend while I was avoiding sugar. They really hit the chocolate spot. And they are so easy and fast! The credit goes to triumphwellness.com.

1½ cups walnuts
Pinch sea salt
13 -14 large dates, pitted
⅓ cup unsweetened cocoa powder
1 tsp. vanilla extract (you could also use mint, cherry or lemon extract)

Place walnuts and salt in a food processor and process until finely ground. Add remaining ingredients and process until all mixed and uniformly crumbly. With the machine running, add a few drops of water at a time, just until the mass starts to stick together in a big ball. (Better to add too little that too much!)

Roll mixture into balls or press into a square pan and cut into squares. Balls can then be rolled in dried coconut, chopped nuts, or cocoa powder if you wish.

Erin Morel

RHUBARB CRISP

4 cups rhubarb, cut up
1 cup sugar
2 Tbsp. flour
1 egg, slightly beaten
½ cup quick oats
⅓ cup brown sugar
¼ tsp. nutmeg
½ cup flour
¼ stick chilled butter

Combine rhubarb, sugar, flour and eggs. Pour into 8 inch round glass pie pan.

Mix oats, sugar, nutmeg, flour and butter, then spoon on top of rhubarb mixture and cook in microwave set on high for 12 to 14 minutes. Top with whip cream or eat it warm with ice cream.

Cory McCormick

SCOTCH-A-ROO'S or PEANUT BUTTER RICE KRISPIE TREATS

1 cup white corn syrup
1 cup white sugar
1 tsp vanilla
1½ cups peanut butter (creamy or crunchy)
6 cup Rice Krispies
½ small pkg. butterscotch chips
1 small pkg. chocolate chips

Bring corn syrup, sugar and vanilla to a boil. Add peanut butter. Pour mixture over Rice Krispies. Remove from heat and add peanut butter. Pour mixture over Rice Krispies.

Press into greased pan and top with the butterscotch and chocolate chips. Let set, cut and serve.

Sheri Isham

SPRITZ COOKIES

Great-Grandma Bessie Lyons' recipe

2 cups flour
¼ tsp salt
¾ cup butter
½ cup sugar
1 egg yolk
1 tsp. vanilla or almond flavoring

Mix all ingredients. Chill cookie dough. Fill cookie press with dough with your favorite shapes. Bake at 375° for 8 to 10 minutes.

Cory McCormick

STRAWBERRY ICEBOX CAKE

12 oz. box vanilla wafers
¾ stick margarine or butter, melted
1 stick margarine or butter
1½ cups sugar
½ cup eggbeaters
2 qts. strawberries, sliced
2 envelopes Dream Whip or 1 pt. whipping cream, whipped

Crush vanilla wafers fine; mix with melted margarine or butter. Spread ¾ of the crumb mixture firmly in a 9 x 13-inch pan. Cream butter or margarine with sugar; add egg beaters; beat well. Spread evenly over crumbs. Add berries. Spread Dream Whip or whipping cream over berries. Sprinkle remaining crumbs over top. Refrigerate overnight.

Jean Berry

Two delicious sugar cookie recipes: you be the judge!

A GREAT SUGAR COOKIE

1 cup butter or margarine
1 cup vegetable oil
1 cup sugar
1 cup confectioners' sugar
2 eggs

1½ tsp. vanilla
4 cups flour
1 tsp. salt
1 tsp. cream of tartar
1 tsp. baking powder

Cream margarine, oil and sugars in a large bowl. Mix together dry ingredients and blend into creamed mixture. Drop by heaping teaspoonfuls onto ungreased cookie sheet. Press down with a whisk. Sprinkle with granulated sugar before and after baking. Bake at 350° for 12 to 15 minutes or until cookies begin to brown lightly.

Nancy Tuberty

SUGAR COOKIES

1 cup butter, room temperature
2/3 cup sugar
1 egg
1 tsp. pure vanilla extract
1 tsp. pure almond extract
½ tsp. salt

2½ cups all-purpose flour, plus more for dusting work surface
1½ cups confectioners' sugar
1+ Tbsp. milk
Food coloring

Mix butter and sugar with electric mixer at medium speed. Beat in egg, vanilla and almond extract. In separate bowl combine flour and salt, then stir (I mix with mixer) into butter mixture. Cover dough with plastic wrap and chill for 30 min. Roll out on surface and use cookie cutters. Bake at 350° for 8 to 9 minutes. You don't want them to brown. For icing, add 1 tablespoon of milk at a time to confectioners' sugar until a good consistency is reached. Add food coloring. Once cooled, dip tops of cookies into icing and lay out until icing hardens.

Ashley Blackburn

WALDORF ASTORIA CAKE

This is the original red velvet cake recipe from the Waldorf Astoria hotel in New York

½ cup shortening
1½ cup sugar
Pinch of salt
2 eggs
2 oz. bottle red food coloring
1 tsp. vanilla
2 tsp. cocoa
2½ cups cake flour
1 cup buttermilk
1 tsp. baking soda
1 tsp. vinegar

Cream shortening, sugar and salt. Add eggs and continue to beat thoroughly. Add and beat red food coloring, vanilla and cocoa. Then alternating, add flour and buttermilk until fully incorporated. Mix baking soda with vinegar and fold into mixture. Divide batter into three round cake pans and bake at 350° for 30 minutes.

Sheri Isham

A brief history of the Catholic Church in Williamson County, Tennessee

ST. PHILIP CHURCH

Williamson County and Franklin were established simultaneously, in the fall of 1799. As the county seat, Franklin enjoyed rapid growth as settlers from North Carolina and other points east poured into what was then the western frontier. However, there were few Catholics among them. The first Catholic Mass in Franklin was celebrated about 1820 when Kentucky missionary priest Fr. Robert Abell celebrated Mass for two Catholics families in town. While Tennessee's Catholic population was paltry, Kentucky, on the other hand, had a relatively large one. A writer noted that Tennessee's "inland location and peculiar civil history" prevented it from profiting by the tide of immigration that would lead to a larger Catholic population.

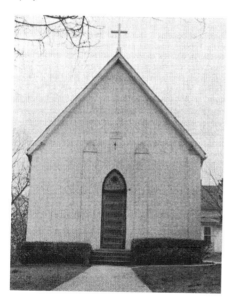

Tennessee was thus part of the diocese of Kentucky, headquartered at Bardstown, until the diocese of Tennessee was established in 1837. Although Bishop Miles took the first step to build a church in Franklin in 1847, when he purchased land for the church, groundbreaking did not occur until 1871.

The 1871 St. Philip Church

One of the greatest missionaries to Tennessee was the Dominican Father James Aloysius Orengo, who was born in Italy in 1820. Father Orengo arrived in Franklin in 1871. By that time, more Catholics had settled in town, and a church was badly needed.

Father Orengo's health failed and the church was completed by Father Francis Thomas Marron, who oversaw the final stages of work and was the first pastor of St. Philip Church. But because there was no rectory, the church was officially a mission, not a parish. Numerous priests served the church during this time, including Father Eugene Gazzo, who recorded the first baptism in Franklin, in 1872, and a group of seven Precious Blood priests from Ohio who served six mission stations.

Fr. Eugene Gazzo

St. Philip was named a parish in 1898, one year after the arrival of Father John A. Nolan. Father Nolan designed, and with the assistance of the parishioners, built a rectory. A talented wood carver, he carved the frames on the Stations of the Cross that may still be seen in the 1871 church today. One notable priest during this time was Father John Hardeman, the first Williamson County native ordained to the priesthood. Father Hardeman converted to the Faith during his service in the Spanish-American War.

During the Great Depression and WWII, declining numbers meant the church could no longer support a resident priest and St. Philip became a mission church again. St. Philip was restored to parish status in 1946 with the arrival of WWII veteran Father Francis J. Reilly. He was succeeded after two years by Father Joseph Cunningham, who was followed by his nephew Father Allan Cunningham from 1962 to 1971.

Fr. John Hardeman

Father Allan Cunningham's tenure at St. Philip was marked by rapid growth, expanding from 11 to over 200 families. The trend continued under Fathers James Miller, John Henrick and Edward Arnold.

The first major expansion was a new sanctuary facing 2nd Avenue, followed by a third and fourth sanctuary and other additions. The current sanctuary, dedicated in 1997, seats 1,000.

Associate pastor John Kirk served after Father Arnold's death as parish administrator. Current pastor Father Bala Showraiah Marneni has served this dynamic, growing parish of 1,600 families since 2009, completing major renovations to the original church and religious education buildings, and adding numerous ministries. He is assisted by associate pastor Father Tien Tran. Father Louis Rojas serves the area's active Hispanic population of about 300 families, celebrating Sunday mass at St. Philip.

ST. MATTHEW CHURCH

St. Matthew Catholic Church was founded in 1978, drawing its initial membership from both St. Philip in Franklin and St. Henry's in Bellevue, which had both become overcrowded. Bishop James Niedergeses selected Father Albert Seiner to become pastor of the new church. First meeting in a Presbyterian church, then a school, the community built its first building, dedicated on May 10, 1981 by Bishop Niedergeses. The new church held 300 people and also had space for religious education classes and Father Seiner's living quarters.

Father Paul Hostettler succeeded Father Seiner as pastor of St. Matthew in 1981. He in turn was followed, in 1987, by Father Luzerne "Lu" Schnupp. Through the continued efforts of parishioners, the mortgage on the original "foundation" building was retired and a substantial amount raised toward the projected cost of the new church, which was completed in 1992. The church also established the first Catholic school in more than 40 years in the diocese of Nashville.

Father Lu retired in 2001. Fr. Andrew Abraham became acting administrator until Father Mark Beckman was assigned to St. Matthew as Pastor in 2002. One year later, Father Mark Hunt arrived as a priest in residence and in 2007 was appointed to Associate Pastor, serving until 2008. He was succeeded by Father Nicholas Allen as Associate Pastor.

The Sisters of Mercy have been a vital part of the community since its early days. Sr. Mary Bernadelle Nolan served from 1988 to 1992 as Parish Minister visiting members of the church community in need. Sr. Mary Thomasetta Mogan served from 1992 to 1998 as Parish Minister and Director of Religious Education. Sr. Lauren Cole is the current Director of Religious Education.

Father Mark Beckman continues to lead a vital and energetic parish meeting the spiritual needs of his church family with over 75 parish ministries serving 1,250 families. He also administers the business affairs of a continually growing parish and school. With the completion of construction in 2005, the parish that began in a borrowed church continues to joyfully celebrate the amazing sense of community that has been created among its people.

HOLY FAMILY CHURCH

In 1989, in response to continued growth and overcrowding at St. Philip, Bishop Niedergeses announced a new parish for Brentwood, naming Father Edward T. Alberts as the pastor. On August 6, 1989, Fr. Alberts celebrated the first community-wide Mass in the Brentwood High School auditorium. First known simply as Brentwood Catholic Community, the parishioners later chose the name Holy Family Catholic Church. With close to 300 registered families and over 400 students in the Religious Education program, the parish was up and running.

In October, 1989, the church's planning committee began to set priorities and plan for the future. Over the next two years, the Commission developed a Parish Mission Statement, a parish

Covenant (By-laws), and looked for a suitable tract of land on which to build the church, eventually purchasing the current property on Crockett Road.

The parish broke ground on the property on Crockett Road in September, 1992. The first phase included the worship area, gathering area, devotional chapel, education wing and administrative offices.

In May, 1999, construction of the parish activity center, including a gym, commercial kitchen, nursery, Life Teen youth room, youth minister's office, and several rooms for religious education classes and various meetings, completed the second phase. Additional building projects include a smaller chapel for weekday Mass, smaller weddings and funerals, and various other liturgies. The picnic pavilion was erected with the proceeds from the Men's Club fundraisers. Behind the picnic pavilion is a baseball diamond and soccer field.

Father Alberts continues as the church's founding pastor after 24 years. Father Titus Augustine serves as associate pastor. Under the guidance of the Spirit, much has been accomplished and many lives touched by God's love through the care and concern of so many dedicated and life-giving people.

CHURCH OF THE NATIVITY

By 2008, rapid growth in the southern part of the Williamson County, drove the decision to form a new parish serving those living in Thompson's Station and Spring Hill. In June, 2008, Bishop David Choby named Father John Kirk pastor of a church to be established in Spring Hill. Thus Church of the Nativity was born.

Because funding a new building in a growth area is an expensive prospect, the church currently meets in a shopping center that has been reconfigured to meet the needs of the parish. A worship center, religious education classrooms, administrative offices and a separate rectory all required major funding, even before a more permanent home could be considered.

Father Kirk notes, "This is the Lord's work! He wills and wants it because of His great love and mercy. He gives us the means to participate in His works. We pray that all of us will listen and respond to the Lord's inspirations and graces to support the parish over the years. Generations to come will benefit from this parish as we all have benefited from parishes that have served for generations."

These inspiring words apply to our seminarians as well. Thank you for helping to support their education by purchasing this cookbook. Won't you continue to do so? Please make an additional donation by sending your check in any amount to:

SERRA Club
c/o St. Philip Church
113 2nd Avenue, South
Franklin, TN 37064

Index

BEVERAGES

Awesome Iced Tea Punch   9
Egg Nog   9
Fruit Tea   11
Michelle's Vodka Slush   10
Mocha Punch   10
Sangria   11
Whiskey Sour Slush   12

APPETIZERS

Artichoke-Cheese Puffs   13
Auntie Ann's Copycat Pretzels   14
Baked Zucchini   26
Black Bean Salsa   14
Bread and Butter Pickles   15
Cheddar Cheese Ball   13
Cowboy Caviar   16
Crab Spread   15
Cream Cheese and Pineapple Ball   16
Fiesta Bean Salad or Dip   17
Goat Cheese-Pear Pancetta Crisps   17
Hummus with a Twist   18
Kielbasa Bites   19
Meme's Cheese Ball   20
MJ's Southwestern Layered Dip   20
Mushrooms   19
Pam's Dip 2-1-1-1-1-1   21
Party Meatballs   21
Pop Joe's Granola   21
Remoulade Sauce   22

Rosemary Crackers   24
Sensational Stuffed Mushrooms   22
Spinach and Mushroom on Crostini   23
Trail Mix   24
Vidalia Onion Dip   25
Vietnamese Egg Rolls   25

BREADS

Biscotti   27
Banana Bread   28
Coffee Cake   28
Coffee Crescents   29
Corn Bread Muffins   30
Fool Proof Southern Biscuits   30
Irish Soda Bread   31
Pineapple Turnovers   32
Poteca   33
Stir and Bake Rolls   34
St. Philip Men's Cub St. Valentine's Day Breakfast for the Ladies Biscuits   35

BRUNCH

Benedictine Sandwiches   37
Cranberry Apple Casserole   38
Egg and Ham Brunch   38
Fr. Kirk's Oatmeal Breakfast   42
French Toast Casserole   40
Ham and Cheese Casserole   40
Hashbrown Quiche   44
Kentucky Hot Brown Casserole   41
Louisville Garlic Cheese Grits   41
Night Before French Toast   39
Overnight Caramel French Toast   39
Quiche   42
Quiche Lorraine   44
Spinach Quiche   43

Sausage Crescent Rolls   45
Sunrise Casserole   45

SOUPS

Cheesy Bakes Potato Soup   47
Chicken Taco Soup   48
Chicken Tortilla Soup   49
Corn and Chicken Soup   49
Cream of Broccoli Soup   50
Creamy Southwestern Pumpkin Soup   51
Gazpacho   51
Hearty Italian Soup   52
Meatless Chili   53
Sopa de Tortilla   54
Pot Liquor Soup   55
Red Bean Soup   50
Sausage-Tortellini Soup   56
Vegetable and Meatball Soup   57
Wedding Soup   58
White Bean Chicken Chili   59
White Chicken Chili   58
Yummy Crock Pot Baked Potato Soup   60

SALADS

Beef Asparagus Salad   61
Chicken Pasta Salad   62
Chicken Salad with Artichokes   62
Chicken Tortellini Pasta Salad   63
Crab and Artichoke Orzo Salad   64
Eleven Layer Salad   65
Fruit Salad   65, 66
Garden Salad   66
Honey Mustard Salad Dressing   67
Italian Pasta Salad   67
Honey Poppy Seed Pasta Salad   68
Honey Ginger Vinaigrette   69

Joanne's Broccoli Salad   69
Kay Dozier's Potato Salad   73
Lemon-Artichoke Chicken Salad   70
Make Ahead Marinated Broccoli-Cauliflower Salad   70
Mixed Greens with Feta and Dried Cranberries   71
MJ's Oriental Chicken and Spinach Salad   72
Quinoa Salad with Dried Fruits and Nuts   74
Red Potato Salad   73
Red Raspberry Salad   71
Seasoned Slaw   77
Sister-in-Law Salad   75
Spinach and Strawberry Salad with Wisconsin Gouda Cheese   76
Spinach Salad with Bacon Dressing   77
Summer Pasta Salad   78
Tomato Mozzarella Salad   78

VEGETABLES AND SIDE DISHES

Bettie's Green Bean Casserole   80
Brown Rice   80
Candied Carrots   81
Carole's Colorado Beans   81
Cheese or Garlic Grits   82
Corn Casserole   82
Corn Pudding   83
Corn Souffle   83
Cream Cheese Basil Summer Squash   95
Dito D'Oro (Oven-fried Eggplant)   84
Eggplant Parmesan   85
Fresh Cranberry Mold   87
Grilled Onion   84
Marinated Asparagus   87
Mac and Cheese   88
Macaroni and Cheese 89
Orzo with Parmesan and Basil   88
Mexican Rice   89
Microwave Spinach Casserole   90
Mission Inn Potatoes   91
Onion Bread Puddings   90

Orange-Pecan Green Beans   92
Overnight Asparagus Strata   79
Potato Casserole   93
Ratatouille   94
Roasted Harvested Vegetables   93
Squash Casserole   94
Spinach, Rice and Feta Pie   95
Strebel Family German Potato Salad   86
Sweet Onion Casserole   97
Sweet Potato Casserole   96
Sweet and Sour Green Beans   96
Yum Yum Yams   97
Zucchini Bordelaise   98
Zucchini, Squash and Tomatoes   98

PASTA

Chicken Tortellini   99
Bow Tie Pasta   100
Lasagna   103
Lupini   100
Orecchiette with Mini Chicken Meatballs   107
Pancit Canton (Stir-fried Noodles)   105
Pizza and Marinara Sauce   106
Spaghetti Ring   108
Spinach Lasagna   104
The Best Lasagna Ever   101

MAIN COURSES

Poultry

Baked Chicken and Rice with Black Beans   109
Baked Crunchy Onion Chicken   110
Balsamic Chicken   110
Caramelized Chicken with Cranberry Conserve   111
Chicken or Pork Adobo or Mix   112

Chicken Almond Casserole   113
Chicken Broccoli Carrot Casserole   113
Chicken and Noodles   114
Chicken Lickin' Casserole   115
Cilantro Lime Chicken   115
Cranberry Chicken   116
Curry Chicken   116
Enchiladas Verdes de Pollo   117
Favorite Bring-to-New-Mama Chicken Pot Pie   118
Janie's Hug Casserole   118
New England Pot Pie   119
Oven Baked Chicken Fajitas   120
Parmesan Chicken   119
Parmesan Crusted Bruschetta Chicken   121
Pollo al Pomodoro   121
Poppy Seed Chicken   122
Quick Chicken Cacciatore   114
Slow Cooker Chicken with Olives   123
Spicy Chicken and Vegetable Stir Fry with Thai Basil   124
Sweet Sour Chicken   120
Tandoori Chicken   126
Turkey and Wild Rice Stew   122
Unstuffed Pepper Casserole   127

Pork

Barbara's Roast Pork Tenderloin   129
Gorton 129
Gourmet Pork Chops   128
Jack Daniel's Pork Tenderloin   130
Jerk Ribs   130
Pork Normandie   131
Pork Roast   132
Stuffed Pork Loin   133
Tuscan Pork Roast   132

Beef

Beef and Gravy   135
Beef Brisket with Whipped Potatoes and Asparagus   136
Bistro Skillet Steak   134
Bride's Meat Loaf   135
Brisket with Portobello Mushrooms and Dried Cranberries   137
Gerry's Meatloaf   138
Grandma's Bar-B-Q Beef   138
Hamburger Casserole   139
Italian Beef   139
Italian Pot Roast   140
Layered Beef and Cabbage Casserole   141
Marinade for Flank Steak   141
No-Peek Stew   142
Rice and Beef Porcupines   142
Stuffed Peppers   143

Lamb

Lamb Stew in a Loaf   144

Seafood

Bahian Halibut   146
Barbeque Shrimp with Jambalaya Sauce   147
Brown Sugar-Glazed Salmon   150
Low Country Boil   148
Orange Roughy in Scallion and Ginger Sauce   149
Salmon Burgers   150
Salmon Fillets   149
Salmon in a Bundle   152
Sesame-Crusted Salmon with Honey-Ginger Vinaigrette   151
Shrimp and Grits   153
Tilapia and Florentine Alfredo Pasta   154

DESSERTS

A Great Sugar Cookie   192
Amish Apple Pie   156
Apple Betty Pie   157
Apricot Nectar Cake   157
Aunt Betty's Peanut Butter Balls with Chocolate Dip   155
No-Bake Apple Pie   158
Barb's Chocolate Cake   162
Bishop Whipple's Pudding   159
Carrot Cake with Cream Cheese Frosting   160
Cherry Delight   164
Chocolate Peanut Candy   163
Chunky Apple Walnut Cake   161
Coconut Pound Cake   164
Coconut Crunch Delight   165
Coconut-Almond Macaroons   166
Cranberry Walnut Torte   167
Delicious Homemade Hot Fudge   167
Éclair Cake   170
Easy Caramel Rolls   169
Easy Peach Cobbler I   168
Easy Peach Cobbler II   168
Flan Napolitano   171
Frozen Chocolate Mousse   169
Frozen Strawberry Dessert   166
Gingerbread Boy Cookies   172
Golden Orange Dreamsicle Cake   173
Heavenly Hash   174
Holiday Pie   174
Jeff's Cookies   175
Lemon Cheese Torte   176
Lemon Sponge Pudding   177
Luscious Lemon Ring   177
Mama's Sweet Saltines   178
Microwave Fudge   179
Molasses Cake   180
My Mom's Old-Fashioned Rice Puddings   179
Oatmeal Cake   181
Oatmeal Chocolate Chip Cookies   182

Oatmeal Raisin Cookies   181
Outstanding Fudge Pie   178
Peach Pie   183
Pecan Pie Bars   184
Pecan Pie   185
Peitzels   185
Pineapple and Marshmallow Pudding   186
Pumpkin Pound Cake with Buttermilk Glaze   187
Pumpkin Roll   188
Raw Brownie Bites   189
Rhubarb Crisp   190
Rich Chocolate Cake   165
Scotch-A-Roos or Peanut Butter Rice Krispie Treats   190
Sprite Cookies   191
Strawberry Icebox Cake   191
Sugar Cookies   192
Waldorf Astoria Cake 193

Made in the USA
Charleston, SC
16 May 2013